The National Gardening Association

A Complete Guide
for Teachers,
Parents and
Youth Leaders

**by Lynn Ocone
with Eve Pranis**

National Gardening Association
Burlington, Vermont

Guide to Kids' Gardening

WILEY

Wiley Science Editions
John Wiley & Sons, Inc.
New York • Chichester • Brisbane • Toronto • Singapore

Acknowledgements

Special thanks to the following people, who each in their own special way, helped to make the *Guide to Kids' Gardening* a reality:

Lee Barr, John Smith, Linda Lutz, Kit Anderson, Heather Hale, Ted Unkles, Carol Peralta, Nancy Flinn, National Gardening Association Youth Garden Grant Recipients, Janice and Abe Burnstein, and the more than 1,300 National Gardening Association members who helped fund the book.

Also, Sheryl Felty, Ruth Page, Barbara Godfrey, Peter Jeffrey, Lois D'Arcangelo, Nina Aiston, Liz Miles, Louise Constantino, Roger Moyer, Lila Achison Wallace, Tommy Thompson, Lyman Wood, Joseph Kiefer, Gary Appel, Jack Hale, Jean Douglas and the Wallace Genetic Foundation. And to all the youth garden leaders across the country who have given help, inspiration and permission to share their work and experiences with others.

Credits

Editor: George Thabault
Technical writer: Larry Sommers
Design: Anthony Sini
Illustrations: Elayne Sears

Revised Edition
Research and writing: Eve Pranis
Project Manager: Larry Sommers

Second printing, 1984.
Revised Edition, 1987.
John Wiley & Sons edition, 1990.

Ocone, Lynn.
The National Gardening Association Guide to Kids' Gardening—John Wiley & Sons ed., by Lynn Ocone with Eve Pranis.
p. cm.—(Wiley science editions)
Rev. ed. of: The youth gardening book, © 1983.
Includes bibliographical references.

ISBN 0-471-52092-6

1. Children's gardens—Handbooks, manuals, etc. 2. Vegetable gardening—Handbooks, manuals, etc. I. Pranis, Eve. II. Ocone, Lynn. Youth gardening book. III. National Gardening Association (U.S.) IV. Title. V. Title: Guide to kids' gardening. VI. Series.
SB457.024 1990   89-48993
635'.083'4—dc20   CIP
Printed in the United States of America.
90 91 10 9 8 7 6 5 4 3 2 1

Publisher's Letter

The *Guide to Kids' Gardening* is our answer to calls and letters from people all over the country asking how to start a garden project for the youngsters they teach, live with, or work with. A few generations ago, such inquiries would never have been made. Then, if youngsters weren't growing food at school, they were surely working in the family garden. Whether or not the gardening experience was enjoyable and opened children's eyes to the majesty and intricacy of nature, one thing was certain: they learned how to garden.

Today, a regrettably large number of children pass through family life and their school years without turning one shovelful of rich, loamy garden soil or planting a single seed. As a teacher mentions in this book, too many children think the "food chain" is a string of supermarkets.

"That's why we've devoted so much energy in recent years to letting dedicated adults know about good youth gardens and how to start yet another one. We know from hundreds of examples that "gardens grow children." A good youth garden isn't just for learning the techniques of food growing. It's also a place for mysteries and discoveries, for talking and singing, for making friends of plants, the earth and fellow gardeners."

The principal author of this book, Lynn Ocone, while she was the National Gardening Association's Director of Youth Gardening Programs, invested much time in learning from our local youth projects. She also gained wisdom and perspective from visits to other projects around the country. Her background in environmental communications and her dedication to gardening education helps make this book highly relevant to the interests of youth leaders. Eve Pranis, researcher and writer for the Revised Edition, is a graduate of Cornell University College of Agriculture and Life Sciences. She has been the director of an extensive garden program for an educational foundation and has done writing and program management at the National Gardening Association.

Since its publication in 1983, we have received many favorable comments from youth leaders who find the *Guide to Kids' Gardening* a most valuable resource. Inquiries from potential garden leaders and reports of new youth gardening programs continue to reach us regularly.

In response to the heightened interest in youth gardening programs and with a firm belief that gardens promote active learning and grow healthy, caring and inquisitive adults, the National Gardening Association is committed to greatly expanding our work in this area. We are making available the information, technical assistance and products that you, the teacher or leader, need to run a successful program.

In revising this book, we were pleased to find that most of the programs are still going strong. In this edition we have added highlights from a number of exciting new programs and have included the most current information on new project ideas, resources, fundraising, management, educational activities and much more.

We hope everyone who receives this book will put it to use, or put it into a youth leader's hands. We hope those of you who so generously contributed time, information and money to make publication of this book possible, find our efforts worthwhile.

We hope you'll continue to help us bring the excitement and rewards of youth gardening into the lives of thousands of boys and girls.

Charles Scott
President
National Gardening Association

CONTENTS

Foreword by Pete Seeger vi
Why Youth Gardening? viii

CHAPTER 1 THE SIX BASIC CHALLENGES x
Leadership 1
Land 3
Money 4
Vandalism 10
Continuity 12
Motivation 13

CHAPTER 2 PLANNING FOR SUCCESS 16
Checklist for a successful youth garden 17
Calendars for year-round programs 22
Plan a harvest party 28

CHAPTER 3 DEVELOPING YOUR SITE 29
Choosing the right site 30
Sprucing up your site 33
Tips on soil testing 34
Topsoil formula 35
Turn over your land early 36
Fertilize regularly 37
Composting 41
Cover crops 42
Does your site require a fence? 43
Getting water to your garden 43
Extend your season with coldframes 45

CHAPTER 4 DESIGNING THE GARDENS 47
Site designs that work 48
Ideas for open space 53
Individual garden layouts 55
Marking plots 58
A plan for 72 kids in the garden 58
Raised beds 61
Signs capture the spirit of your garden 62

CHAPTER 5 THE FUN OF GARDENING. 63
Garden activities for fun and knowledge 65
28 garden experiments and tests 66
Garden activities 70

The Garden Journal 70
Find the Hidden Words 70
Garden Riddles .71
Garden Jeopardy 72
World Hunger Activity 73
Build a Home for Your Praying Mantis . . .74
Where Does Food Come From? 75
Watch Roots Grow 76
Pickle a Big Cucumber in a Bottle 76
Recycle Some Garbage 77
Flower Dissection 78
Story Hour 79
Zig-Zagging Seed 80
The Mysterious Feely Box 80
Special T-Shirts for Everyone 81
Colorful, Waterproof Row Markers 81
Make a Toad House 82
Blackberry Jamming. 83
Build a Japanese Beetle Trap 84
Grow Your Name on a Pumpkin 84
Naming the Biggest, Smallest and Most
Interesting 85
Grow Plants in a Maze 85
Natural Blueprints from the Garden. 86
Brewing Solar Mint Tea 87
Catch the Raccoon's Tail 87

Plant Corn, Beans, and Squash in a
Mound 88
Making a Solar Food Dryer 89
A Little Care for Your Tools 90
Making Manure Tea Fertilizer 90
Keeping Growth Charts 91
The Rain Gauge 91
Homemade Insect Spray 92
Garden Skits and Charades 92
Raising Worms .93
Vegetable Designs 94
Sensory Awareness. 94
Concentration 95
Weed Salads 96
Collecting Insects from Your Garden 97
Making a Plant Press 98
Bean Thrashing. 99
Bird Feeders 100
Crafting a Corn Husk Doll 101
Corn Grinding and Patty Making. 102
A Dazzling Carrot Necklace 103
Making Veggie Creatures 103
Drying Flowers 104
Grinding Wheat Berries into Flour 106
Learning about Seed Production 107
Sing a Song 108
Some other activity ideas 109

CHAPTER 6 THE BASICS OF INDOOR GARDENING AND
CONTAINER GARDENING 110
Indoor gardening techniques 111
Growing plants to harvest — indoors 115
Container gardening. 117

CHAPTER 7 A WORLD OF YOUTH GARDENS 122
People and organizations behind youth gardens 123
Youth Garden Portraits. 130

RESOURCES. 139

INDEX 146

A Message About Kids and Gardening from Pete Seeger*

It's a miracle. A little seed—planted, sprouts, grows. In due time it's a flower or something good to eat, or both.

It's a miracle. A bunch of ordinary kids. No geniuses. A little guidance, some natural energy, and some careful attention. One person alone couldn't do it. But together we can. We, a mixed bag of personalities, hang-ups and hopes. We. A miracle.

Some people don't believe in miracles. They say there's no hope for this world. The evil people have all the power. But green miracles are growing all around them. Rainbow miracles surround them. Surround their lies and make their lies sound silly.

Sun and rain. Ancient miracles more extraordinary than anything else in the world. Life, life, life, pushing up. Put manure on, it grows all the better. Get worms to help.

And in distant future times children will read in their history books how in the 20th Century many thought the world would be destroyed by war or hate or misdirected science. But everyone in the world started gardening again. They re-learned some old lessons:

How much fun it is to garden. How home-grown things taste better. How wonderful it is to share. How satisfying it is to work hand in hand with miracles.

Pete Seeger

*Editor's note: Pete Seeger, who often sings the "Garden Song" (p. 108) at concerts, reviewed *The Youth Gardening Book* and called it "a real encyclopedia of knowledge." His wife, Toshi, does most of their home gardening so we invited them to write a message for this book.

WHY YOUTH GARDENING?

Environmental stewardship

We all, as the stewards of the planet, must be aware of our role in the environment and to begin to seek long-term solutions to environmental problems. Through gardening, children actively learn about interdependent plant and animal needs, about complex natural cycles and webs, and about their own roles as responsible caretakers. These experiences lay the groundwork for making responsible environmental choices as adults.

Multidisciplinary, active learning

Gardening enlivens learning by offering a hands-on approach to seeking information and to learning skills and concepts. Children become observers, questioners, doers and problem solvers. While science and ecology might be the obvious garden subjects, consider the exciting possibilities for using the garden as a springboard for teaching math, reading, writing, social studies and art.

Personal growth/social skills

Nurturing plants from seed to harvest inevitably leads to increased feelings of confidence, self-esteem and pride. One need only see the beaming face of a child who has harvested her first carrot to appreciate the value of this experience. The child becomes empowered and motivated by the realization that hard work and patience produce concrete, satisfying results.

The garden provides a place for groups of youngsters to cooperate, solve problems together and share the fruits of their labor. As the skills of problem-solving and cooperation are so tenuous globally, this experience is a critical one for our future leaders.

SHOOTS 'N ROOTS, MILWAUKEE, WISCONSIN

Nutrition/Health

Gardening promotes physical health and is a valuable vehicle for teaching lessons about food and nutrition. It can enable children to make food choices based on new tasting experiences and increased appreciation and understanding of where our food comes from.

MARK RENKEL

Community improvement

Youth gardens not only beautify and transform the school or club environment, but allow children to become actively involved in improving their own communities. Members of the community, in turn, respond with increased local pride and support for the gardening efforts.

Hunger and other social concerns

The garden sets the stage for discussing, investigating and responding to local and global food and hunger issues. Issues concerning food production, food distribution, agricultural technology and land resources can be integrated into the garden program. This experience offers children the opportunity to actively address some of these problems locally and realize that they can be part of the solution.

It's fun! And a practical skill

Above all, gardening is *fun* and is a skill that, once acquired, can be a lifelong companion. It is not a skill that must be mastered to be enjoyed, and it is extremely adaptable to diverse needs and abilities.

For some children gardening may offer merely the excitement of watching seeds grow and harvesting the bounty. For others it offers the opportunity to develop skills they would build on as adults, leading possibly to a rewarding hobby or career.

Metrics in the Garden

A lot of gardening entails measuring...the width to plant rows, the distance apart and the depth to set seedlings, how much water and fertilizer to use, the temperature, and the quantity of your harvest. With all that measuring, gardening becomes a perfect opportunity to become metrically literate!

Here is some useful information to convert from English to metric measurements in the garden:

Length

inch = 2.54 centimeters

foot = 0.3048 meter

yard = 0.9144 meter

centimeter = 0.3937 inch

meter = 3.2808 feet

meter = 1.0936 yards

To convert:

When you know the length, for example, the number of inches, multiply by 2.54 to get the total number of centimeters:

16 in. x 2.54 cm/in. = 40.64 cm

Volume

cubic inch = 0.0164 liter

cubic foot = 28.3162 liters

cup = 0.2366 liter

quart = 0.9463 liter

gallon = 3.7853 liters

teaspoon = 4.93 milliliters

tablespoon = 14.79 milliliters

liter = 61.0250 cubic inches

liter = 0.0353 cubic foot

liter = 0.2642 gallon

liter = 1.0567 quarts

liter = 1000 milliliters

fluid ounce = 29.57 milliliters

Mass

ounce = 28.3495 grams

pound = 454 grams

pound = 0.4536 kilogram

gram = 0.0353 ounce

kilogram = 2.2046 pounds

Cropping Yield

lbs./sq. ft.	kg./sq. m.
1.0	4.9
1.4	6.8
2.0	9.8
2.2	10.8
2.6	12.7
3.0	14.7

Temperature

°C	°F
0	32
5	41
10	50
15	59
20	68
25	77
35	95
40	104

Fahrenheit to Centigrade
$5/9 \ (°F - 32) \times °C$

Centigrade to Fahrenheit
$9/5 \ (°C) + 32 \times °F$

FREE Six-Month Membership
in the National Gardening Association

JOIN US!

And become one of the 200,000 gardeners from coast to coast who receive *National Gardening* magazine.

Cut out and return this coupon to:

**NATIONAL GARDENING ASSOCIATION
DEPT. JWS
180 FLYNN AVENUE
BURLINGTON, VT 05401-9969**

YES! Sign me up as a member of the National Gardening Association, with a free six-month subscription to *National Gardening* magazine.

Name_____

Address_____

City_____ State_____ ZIP_____

☐ I want to learn more about kids' gardening. Please send me additional information.

Limited to new subscribers. Send no money,
BUT PLEASE RETURN THIS COUPON TODAY.
THIS OFFER GOOD ONLY FOR RESIDENTS OF
THE UNITED STATES.

CHAPTER 1 | THE SIX BASIC CHALLENGES

Nothing teaches like experience. And the experiences of youth garden leaders have taught us that there are six basic challenges to a successful youth garden project.

If you are planning a new youth garden, you probably won't have to face *all* of these challenges. But you can expect two or three of them to be of concern right from the beginning, before you start any detailed planning. And funding and deterring vandalism may become annual challenges, as some experienced garden leaders realize.

The six challenges posed here may be brought up by the people you approach to support your garden project—city officials, school teachers and principals, parents, landowners, etc. We urge you to spend time now determining how you or your group will face them.

1. Leadership .... "Should we go ahead with a garden program if there's no great gardener to lead it?" Page 1

2. Land .... "How can we have a youth garden project when we don't have much land?" Page 3

3. Money .... "How can we start a garden program without much money?" Page 4

4. Vandalism .... "What about vandalism and theft?" Page 10

5. Continuity .... "If a youth garden project is sponsored by our school, how do we manage it through the summer?" Page 12

6. Motivation .... "How do we keep the interest of the young gardeners once everything is planted?" Page 13

1. LEADERSHIP

"Should we go ahead with a garden program if there's no great gardener to lead it?"

Relax. You don't have to be a super green thumb to get a garden project off the ground. Some gardening know-how is important for the person who shows young people "how to do it," but he or she need not be a walking encyclopedia.

"I have helped the grade school students at Condon School till, plant, tend, and harvest a small vegetable garden for the past two years. Gardening teaches timeless truths sorely lacking among this society's young people. You reap what you sow. Everything has its season. The world must be managed carefully. Endeavors are easily destroyed.

"Furthermore, in time of political upheaval, the ability to grow food on a small intensive scale can be invaluable to a population. Finally, to quote Peter Chan's old Chinese proverb, "if you wish to be happy for the rest of your life, become a gardener."

Tom Bettman, volunteer Eugene, Oregon

ELIZABETH F. GAMBLE FD.

Roots and Shoots Intergenerational Garden Program, Palo Alto, CA.

Seniors Offer Help and Share in the Joys of Gardening

Molly Brown and Mary McCullough, coordinators of educational programs at the Elizabeth F. Gamble Garden Center in Palo Alto, California, envisioned and initiated a special youth gardening program. In 1985 they recruited 12 senior volunteers to work with an enthusiastic third grade teacher at Walter Hays Elementary School to establish an intergenerational school garden.

After initial training from a local Cooperative Extension adviser, the 'garden grandmothers' now meet regularly with the class to "explore the wonders of plant growth, garden food webs and to build awareness of our food sources," explains Molly.

Half of each hour-long session is spent working together in the garden while the other half is devoted to instruction about dissecting flowers, propagating plants, making herbal bouquets and many more activities. Further support is offered by a local Master Gardener volunteer who introduces a 'bug of the week' to the class along with a lesson that ties into the garden program.

One of the strongest points of the program, remarks Molly, is that "it brings two generations together in a time of increasing isolation between younger children and older adults. These garden friendships between young and old are fostering positive attitudes toward aging as well as toward youth."

One first-year program leader said, "I almost didn't go ahead with the garden program because of my own fear of failure. Looking back, I'm ashamed to think that my lack of self-confidence almost prevented 30 kids from having this most wonderful experience."

Another organizer told us, "You may not know a lot, but you can rest fairly well assured that you know more than the kids do. Just be honest with them and work out the kinks together."

If you want help planning and carrying out the gardening lessons, ask for it. There are plenty of parents, teachers and neighbors who are excellent gardeners, who understand soil, weather conditions, and insect problems. If you find one or two who are willing to help and who enjoy working with children, you've got it made.

Said Barbara Britz of the Urban Agriculture Program of Eugene, Oregon, "If we all waited for experience, we might never start! In fact, learning together may cause a camaraderie and group spirit that a leader might not instill."

Involve parents and others...you might get the gardening help you need!

Parents and other adults can be a major resource for gardening projects. Here are some ways garden coordinators have found to engage their interest:

*Formally invite parents, adults such as your county Extension agent, garden-related business people, teachers and garden club members to serve on a garden advisory committee. Get the committee started in the initial planning stages so members feel they are part of the program and can help with decisions. If you choose the advisory committee wisely, some members will be able to offer expert help.

*Send a brief newsletter home with kids regularly. Ask for parent assistance, contributions and services.

*Make a schedule of garden class times, and ask parents to sign up for days they can assist. Invite parents to share their special skills, interests and ideas. Even if parents don't garden, they can help in many ways such as offering cooking workshops, helping with crafts, leading field trips, and in nature studies. At one garden, a little girl told about her aunt who dries flowers. The coordinator invited the aunt to do a workshop on flower drying.

*If appropriate, schedule garden meetings twice a week, once in the morning and once in the evening. This gives more working parents the opportunity to get involved.

*Use special events to attract parents and other adults who can't visit regularly. Schedule one or two happenings each season, such as a first planting day, harvest festival, picnic, or fund-raising event.

*In a successful garden, there will be plenty of food to take home to parents. This is one of the best ways to involve parents—showing them "proof of the pudding."

Explore other volunteer possibilities

*Colleges, universities and even high schools can be a good source of volunteer labor. The older students exchange their creativity and time for the opportunity to develop horticultural, teaching and other skills. Approach local educational institutions to determine if they will offer credit to students participating as volunteer interns in your program.

    *Recruit volunteers from a local senior center, garden club or similar organization.

    *Contact your local Cooperative Extension office to find out about their Master Gardener program. In exchange for their horticultural training, these gardeners make a specific commitment to use their new skills as volunteers.

2. LAND

"How can we have a youth garden project when we don't have much land?"

There are youth groups sponsoring basketball teams with no gym of their own, right? Well, it's the same story with gardening. There are several good ways to have a successful youth garden project without much land of your own.

Look around near your home, whether that's a school, Boys' Club, neighborhood agency, or whatever. There may be well-suited open land nearby, perhaps owned by an individual or a business. Outline your project ideas for them and ask for assistance. It certainly doesn't hurt to ask.

Find out where the nearest community garden is. Talk to the garden coordinators and sponsors about land for a youth project. They might be eager for new ideas to bring more involvement and an added dimension to the site.

How about giving the concept of edible landscaping a try? Youngsters can landscape a building site with a varied selection of food-bearing plants, usually perennial vegetables and fruits which don't need too much year-to-year maintenance.

Perhaps a home garden project is the way to go. This idea, usually associated with schools, has been employed successfully for many years in Cleveland and in Winnipeg, Canada. During the school year, youngsters study and experiment with the basics of gardening, but they plant their own individual gardens at home. During the summer, teachers visit and offer some help and instruction. In the Canadian program, judges make one or two visits and award prizes to some of the most productive and creative gardeners when school resumes in the fall.

Perhaps the easiest way to overcome a land handicap is to get into container gardening—using pots, tubs, cans and buckets of all sizes to grow delicious vegetables.

It is easy and exciting to grow many vegetables to maturity in containers indoors under lights. School garden projects sponsored by the Knox Parks Foundation in Hartford, Connecticut, have had tremendous success with indoor gardening.

For practical pointers on container and indoor gardening, see Chapter 6.

3. MONEY

"How can we start a garden program without much money?"

Let's face it—garden projects do cost money, but how much they cost can vary quite a lot.

Many programs offset their expenses by selling produce, or, if it's an institutional program, by using their harvest in the food service kitchen. Most programs have had success soliciting materials and services from local businesses, parents and other community members.

To keep costs low and to extend the base of support, garden projects can be integrated with existing programs that have funding such as 4-H, boys' and girls' clubs, community gardens and school departments. For example, after her first year in the garden, teacher Louise Costantino said, "Next year I'm going to plan my entire plant unit around the garden." As a result, in the garden project's second year, the science budget covered garden teaching materials, while a bake sale and contributions covered the rest of the costs.

For more fund-raising information, see pages 9 and 10.

Tools are largest expense

The major expense for most garden programs is purchasing tools. If tools are of good quality, and get good care, they will last a long time. So, an initial investment in good-quality, durable tools can mean a saving in the long run.

The advantages of buying tools are: 1. you have them from year to year; 2. you have control of the variety and quality of your tools; 3. you are assured of having enough of the right tools.

To make the most of your money, here's a look at a first and second year list of items needed for an outdoor garden program. Keep in mind that not all programs need the same things.

FIRST YEAR
Garden tools: Hoes, rakes, trowels, hand cultivators, garden shovel. Wheelbarrow or garden cart. Garden hose. Sprinklers (or watering cans). Tape measure. Harvesting knives. Garden stakes.

Soil amendments: Fertilizer and lime. Seeds and plants. Activity supplies for garden crafts, starting plants, ecology studies, experiments, etc.

SECOND YEAR
Soil amendments: Fertilizer, lime or sulphur. Seeds and plants. Activity supplies. (Water and soil preparation are services which may have to be paid for each year. Do your best to get them donated before negotiating on prices.)

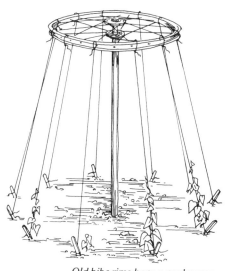

Buy tools which last.

Old bike rims have a garden use.

Save money by cutting garden expenses

1. For trellises and garden stakes use old bicycle rims, tree branches, old ski poles. Says instructor David Evans of Cheraw, South Carolina, "There are many tobacco farmers in our area. Many of them are going to bulk-curing barns and don't need the traditional tobacco sticks anymore. They let us have them for garden stakes."

2. Donated paint stirrers from paint or hardware stores can be used as garden stakes or row markers.

3. If you order a lot of seed from catalogs, take bids from different seed companies. Regional seed companies may sometimes donate seeds to youth garden projects. Write and ask. Tell them about the publicity they'll receive.

4. Many stores will give you seeds or sell them at 50 percent off if you approach them at the end of the selling season. Save seeds in a refrigerator or freezer for the following year if you've already planted your garden.

5. Use plenty of mulch to save on watering bills. Many mulches are free: glass clippings, leaves, newspapers, etc. Also, try to get farmers or horse stable owners to let you have manures free. This will save on fertilizer costs.

6. Finally, as one mother of a young gardener said, "Watch what the kids do in the garden if you want to discover ways to make do or do without. They're the ones who come up with the best ideas."

Budgeting

Following are two sample youth garden program budgets to give you a taste of budgeting possibilities. The expenses and income vary, reflecting the different scope of each program.

Budget A

This sample budget was adapted from several successful garden program budgets. In this case, a school district invested money for site preparation, fencing and other 'start-up' expenses. To insure a long return on its investment, the district hired a full-time garden project coordinator who works with teachers and students to integrate gardening into the school curriculum.

These seedlings are being started for a spring plant sale.

Time of program	Year round
Garden size	1 acre
Youngsters participating	**School year:** 500-600
	Summer: 90-100
Youngsters' time per week	**School year:** 2 hours
	Summer: variable
Number of organizers	1 program coordinator
	12 teachers
Organizers' time per week	**School year:**
	coordinator—40 hours
	teachers—3 hours
	Summer:
	coordinator—40 hours
	teachers/volunteers—40 hours

VIVIENNE DELLA GROTTA

Why Youth Garden Leaders Should Get Paid!

While most youth garden project leaders love gardening and children, this is no reason they should not be paid for their work.

Running a successful youth garden project takes a lot of time, energy, expertise, and often some out-of-pocket expenses. As with all working professionals, garden project leaders deserve to be compensated for their services.

There are many cases of "burnout" among youth garden project leaders, ususally stemming from lack of recognition and financial compensation. A school teacher might volunteer to run a summer garden project for a season or two, but not much longer. Sponsors should recognize the value of the program and make a commitment to fund it.

Across the country, at both elementary and secondary levels, schools (such as James Monroe in Lakewood, California, and Prairie du Chien High in Wisconsin) pay teachers a year-round salary for managing the garden programs.

We commend these institutions and urge others to follow their lead.

YEAR ONE

INCOME
Funds raised by student recycling efforts $400
Produce sales at farmers market 600

Other contributions
In-kind donations of tools, seeds, plants
from parents and local businesses 500
Donation of mulch hay 100
Volunteer time of Cooperative Extension Master Gardeners 1,000

Total Income: $1,000 cash
$1,600 other contributions

EXPENSES
Project coordinator (salary and benefits) $18,000
Materials for renovating greenhouse 1,000
Lumber and materials for tool shed 200
Site preparation (clearing, grading, plowing) 800
Fencing 1,500
Water system 300
Rototiller 500
Hand tools 400
Fruit trees 150
Educational materials/curriculum 200
Soil amendments 200
Planting pots and flats 100
Seeds, plants 200

Total Expenses: $23,550*

YEAR TWO AND FOLLOWING

INCOME
Funds raised by student recycling efforts $600
Spring plant sale 400
In-kind donations of seeds, plants, fertilizer, etc. 300

Total income: $1,000 cash
$300 donated supplies and services

EXPENSES
Project coordinator $18,000
Seeds and plants 200
Soil amendments 200

Total expenses: $18,400*

*Expenses are covered by the school district.

Budget B

This sample budget reflects a school gardening program that can go a long way on little money. Expenses are minimal, the community provides donations and free services, and teachers and parents volunteer their time during the summer.

Time of program .... Year-round
Garden size .... 5,000 square feet
Youngsters participating........................... **School year: 75**
Summer: 10
Number of organizers .... 3 teachers
Organizers' time per week .... **School year: 3 hours each**
Summer: 2 hours each
60 hours total volunteer time for the season

INCOME
Bake sale $100
NGA Garden Grant (tools and seeds) 600
Other Contributions:
    supplies from garden center 100
    tilling services 80
    spreading manure 30
    tools (parents) 100
    mulch hay 100

Total income: $100 cash
$1,010 other contributions

EXPENSES
Curriculum materials $50
Pest controls 25
Mulch 25

Total expenses: $100

Good "PR" can help you get the money you need— every year!

Good public relations makes it a lot easier to approach potential supporters and ask for a donation to help your project. The more good notices you get, the less you have to work to prove your project is worthwhile.

Here are some pointers and recommendations to keep in mind when you think about public relations:

1. Believe in what you're doing. Know the names of all the people involved in starting and supporting the project, and the project's history. Be able to state clearly at any time what is going on and what you want to accomplish.

JOSEPH KIEFER

Keep the media informed of special news-worthy events.

Dedicate Your Garden

An organized, well-publicized dedication or groundbreaking ceremony can create interest, excitement and establish a base of support for your garden effort. Invite local politicians, administrators, school board members, parents, neighbors and of course, the media, to commemorate the new beginning.

In California, the Lodi Unified School District marked the opening of their Life Lab school garden with a Life Lab Arbor Day tree planting celebration while the Happy Valley Primary School added a different twist. Their dedication, complete with a speech by a state senator, ended with the dramatic release of 400 brightly colored helium balloons bearing this message:

> **Dear finder,**
> **This message comes to you from my school, Happy Valley Primary in Anderson, CA. My classmates and I are asking for special help for our science program. We have a science lab and a school garden. We need donations of money, tools, science "stuff" or whatever. We will really appreciate your help.**

2. Keep in touch with supporters and potential supporters by letter, and solicit letters of support from them. They'll come in handy for fund-raising.

3. Make the effort to meet the key people at your local newspaper, TV or radio stations. Treat them as friends of your project; keep them informed, and don't feel bad if they don't cover your project each time you call or write them.

4. Some items the media may be interested in:
   - dedication/groundbreaking ceremony
   - announcement of your project getting under way
   - calls for adult volunteers and participants
   - a large donation from an individual or business
   - first day of working the soil or planting
   - picture session or open house when the garden looks good (often 5-8 weeks after planting)
   - unusual experiments or crops
   - new sign built by youngsters
   - harvest festival
   - market stand near garden

5. Invite local officials to tour your project and coordinate the event with some press coverage. Encourage young gardeners to join you and tell about their garden experiences.

6. Write an occasional letter to the editor of the local paper, or ask someone who supports your efforts to write one. Ask parents of young gardeners to put their comments down on paper.

7. Save color slides of the project and when you have enough, show them to civic groups, the local PTO and teachers' associations, and to people at social agencies.

8. If you have a big project, print up an inexpensive report on the season's activities. Talk about the need for support and give people who read it a way to respond and to make contributions.

9. When the season is over, make sure your garden site is in top condition. Keep it neat and clean. Don't give anyone the chance to run down your efforts because there are untended areas around your garden.

10. If you have surplus vegetables, find a group that needs them and donate the food. If you do this regularly, it's a good story for the media.

Soliciting Donations

Soliciting donations from local groups and businesses is more than a way of obtaining needed money and materials. It serves to publicize and develop support for your program and to actively involve the community in supporting education. There are numerous innovative ways to solicit donations and below are some helpful, basic guidelines.

*Have a specific plan and set of needs in mind before approaching potential donors. Have a list of the particular items that you'd like from each donor.

*You may want to send a preliminary letter, briefly describing your program and asking for an appointment. In any case, make an appointment to talk with the manager or owner in person.

*In the meeting, briefly describe your program (color photos can be a plus) and outline your specific needs. If appropriate, show them a materials list and ask them to donate a few specifics.

*It's critical to tell prospective donors how you'll highlight their donation. In the Milwaukee Urban Garden Program, for instance, contributors are spotlighted on large entrance signs to the community gardens.

*All donations should be followed up with a thank-you letter and contact with donors should be maintained. Send any newspaper clippings or photos that highlight the company's name or materials. Be sure to mention your donors in any news stories, publicity, etc.

Other Funding Sources

While soliciting from individuals and businesses and staging fund-raising events can contribute much-needed materials, services and funds, many youth garden leaders are tapping funding sources which may offer more substantial or more long-term support.

Community development block grants

These funds are allocated by the federal government to U.S. cities to be used according to local needs and priorities. Youth gardening projects are eligible for these grants which may range from $500 to $50,000 for one program. Contact your mayor's office for information and application procedures. Involve the children in the process of securing the funds. They can attend council meetings and write letters to successfully lobby for city block grant money for their gardening program.

Community foundations

Community foundations can be a good source of funding because they provide assistance exclusively to groups in a specific geographic region. They are often a coalition of donors formed to provide a structure for allocating funds to meet community needs. (See: additional contacts, below, for more information.)

Public school foundations

These are sometimes established by private groups to provide financial support to public schools for innovative activities. Grants range in size and may be used by a single teacher or for a program benefiting many classrooms. (See: Additional contacts, below, for more information.)

Adopt-a-school (Adopt-a-garden)

Many states and cities promote partnerships between businesses or the community and public schools through industry councils or other commerce organizations. These programs are intended to promote involvement and interaction between businesses, communities and schools.

The bonuses for the businesses are that by adopting a school or a garden, they can directly affect the quality of the public schools, invest in future leaders and enhance their own image within the community.

In some cases, schools and other programs have drawn up contracts with sponsoring businesses. The company may commit to adopt a program by donating a specified amount of money. This might be supplemented with materials, awards or other assistance. In exchange, the youth program highlights the sponsoring business in various ways. Many have prominent plaques identifying the sponsoring organization

About Tax Deductions...

When talking to individuals and companies about donating money, materials or services, you might hear a lot about tax deductions.

We urge you to become familiar with the broad guidelines of the Internal Revenue Service regarding the kinds of charitable contributions and which are allowed as tax deductions.

Publication 526 ''Charitable Contributions'' and Publication 561 ''Determine the Value of Donated Property'' are available from the IRS and probably have all the information you need.

There are many ways individuals and businesses can help your project and gain tax advantages, but it's important to have a grasp of the basics to get the fund-raising benefit from the tax system.

For example, if an individual allows you to use a plot of land rent-free, can that individual deduct the rental value of the property? (The answer is "no.")

If an individual volunteers a truck and time to haul organic matter to your garden site, what expenses can he or she claim as deductions? (The answer is "gas, oil, tolls, meals while traveling, but not the value of time donated.")

If a nursery donates flats of vegetables at the end of the selling season, can the business claim full retail price for the contribution? (The answer is "only if the merchandise was likely to be sold at full retail price at that time.")

One final point: in order for an individual or business to receive a deduction, the contribution must go to a public charity or institution that has tax-exempt status as determined by the IRS.

A Potpourri of Moneymakers

Many youth garden projects, big or small, grow a little cash along with their vegetables. Here's a list of some money-producing activities we've heard about:

● recycling aluminum, newspaper and office paper ($200-300 per year)
● bake sale ($50-100 each)
● sale of eggs, rabbit meat, piglets, sausage from youth farm project ($2,000-3,000 per year)
● chicken barbecue ($500)
● u-pick sales at high school vegetable gardens ($60-100)
● grade school student and parent paper drive ($500)
● sale of dried flower bouquets, wreaths, herbal sachets and vinegars, pressed flower stationery ($500)
● indoor-grown vegetable, flower and houseplant sales ($200)

and, of course, mention the sponsor in other outreach and publicity. Many such partnerships include other exchanges such as career exploration, classroom speakers, and job shadowing.

To find out if such programs are already established in your area, contact your local chamber of commerce or office of education. If not, consider initiating an 'adopt-a-garden' program.

State Department of Education

There are different state and federal programs established to provide funding for special activities within schools. The science, health or nutrition specialist at your state Department of Education should have information regarding current programs.

Additional contacts

For more information on these and other funding sources contact:
Your local United Way office listed in the phone book, or
The Foundation Center
79 Fifth Avenue
New York, NY 10003
1-800-424-9836

The Foundation Center provides assistance in fund-raising through a nationwide network of reference collections on foundations and corporate donors. The centers are set up at key libraries to provide directories, reports and a free orientation to fund-raisers.

4. VANDALISM

"What about vandalism and theft?"

Many groups hesitate to get involved in youth garden projects for fear vandalism and theft will spoil the experience. Well, whenever anyone has a garden there is the chance for vandalism and theft. But there are ways to drastically reduce the possibility of problems. All those listed here have been used by active programs with some success.

1. One of the best strategies is to involve potential vandals in the program—or even vandals who have been caught. If some youngsters are known as trouble makers in the community, invite them to keep an eye on things. Include them in planning, and in the physical labor of the gardens. Too often young vandals get into trouble simply because they are bored, or sometimes without realizing it, envious. Give them something meaningful to do, and show your appreciation.

2. The more people involved in the program, the better. At school gardens be sure to include classes that do not have gardens. Share food with them, give guided tours, and invite them to your special events.

3. Locate the garden away from main thoroughfares, and as close as you can to the yards of friendly homeowners. Ask neighbors to keep an eye on the garden.

4. Harvest crops as soon as they are ready, or even a little early, so they don't tempt vandals. Don't let red ripe tomatoes sit on the vines.

5. Put signs near the garden letting people know why you have a garden. Signs should list a contact person in case someone wants to have a garden or participate in the program.

6. Youth leaders have mixed opinions about fences. Many believe they just provide a greater challenge for would-be troublemakers. For others, they are very helpful.

7. Tell local police about the garden program and ask them to patrol the garden site regularly.

8. Plant extra seed, grow uncommon varieties, and camouflage tempting veggies such as tomatoes with less inviting crops, such as kale, chard or squash vines.

9. Sprinkle wood ashes, talcum powder or lime over plants during the peak harvest season. Potential thieves might mistake this for mold or insecticides.

10. Establish a frequent, noticeable presence at the site, especially during peak harvest time. You might even schedule parents to patrol the gardens in the evenings until dusk.

11. Plant climbing roses around the fences bordering the area of the youth garden. Scotch Thistle and thorny blackberries also work well to make intruders pay the price.

Some reflections about vandalism and theft from youth garden leaders

"Our garden has been in existence for 11 years—and as long as we don't let vandals take over we'll continue. We repair damage and replant immediately. The vandalism has diminished over the years. Now perhaps once or twice a year our picket fence is broken, but there is no other damage to our gardens.

"We were going to enclose the garden with a stockade fence to keep the garden from the view of outsiders. Our police precinct advised us not to because if vandals were in our garden, no one would see and there would probably be more damage done."

Madaline Gudonsky
Queens Botanical Children's Garden
Flushing, New York

"Unfortunately, a garden and vandalism go hand in hand, especially if the garden is in an area that's visible to a wide audience. A youth garden is worth trying, despite vandalism. Don't let the fear rule you. You might be surprised—there could be less than you think. It's important to explain to adult leaders and participants that vandalism is a real possibility—that it should be expected."

Mary K. Ross
Project Growmaha
Omaha, Nebraska

This sign reduces the possibility of vandalism.

"I was very concerned about a problem with vandalism when we started this program. The Boys' Club is located in a high crime area. What I did was use a piece of land owned by our gardening program leader to have this year's garden. The area is fenced in and private with easy access to water. We haven't had any problems with vandalism."

Patrick Garland
Portage Boys' Club
Ravenna, Ohio

"Garden programs for young people often work the best in areas you least expect them to. Gardens can be the turning point for a community...from vandalism, trash dumping and no sense of community...to a place of beautiful food production, community adventure, a place where kids and adults alike take pride in their neighborhood."

Tommy Thompson
Founder, National Gardening Association
Burlington, Vermont

5. CONTINUITY

"If a youth garden project is sponsored by a school, how can it run through the summer?"

A big obstacle for schools is carrying a garden program through the summer vacation. There are proven ways to get over this hurdle.

Teachers frequently volunteer to carry school garden programs through the summer. But, as mentioned before, experience shows most teachers lose momentum over the years if they are not compensated for their work. So, before depending on volunteers, explore other options.

One alternative is to link the garden program with a summer school program that already exists and is staffed with paid people. School gardens are most easily integrated within year-round or community schools which are a part of the public school system.

Quite often parks and recreation departments use schools during the summer. They might be receptive to expanding their summer program to include gardening, and to paying a part-time coordinator.

The Lincoln School in Lincoln, Vermont, has a garden program which is organized and managed by a teacher during the school year. In summer the Lincoln Sports Summer Camp, a free community camp, takes over responsibility for the garden program.

Another large school garden in Vermont is planted during the school year. During summer, students who want to visit the gardens at the school meet there twice a week with teachers who volunteer their time. Students who are unable to visit the garden, but want to stay involved, can choose to have home gardens. 4-H leaders visit these home gardeners to give support and instruction.

Lincoln School, Vermont

Many schools (even in far Northern states) grow spring salad gardens to harvest before school is out for summer. They also plant crops such as pumpkins and winter squash to harvest when school is back in session. With proper planning and care, the summer garden may require only four or five visits. Students may or may not be involved during the summer. Two things to think about: gardens of this nature are more apt to be vandalized, since they are not tended regularly; youths also easily lose interest in the program because they are not involved during the summer.

Leaving it up to students to visit the summer garden on their own usually results in their losing interest. It's best to have one or two adults responsible for the garden program during the summer and to have a schedule for kids' visits. Other community members can be recruited to help—parents are especially important.

A school garden can be successful in summer when children spend at least 2 hours a week in the gardens. For every 2 hours of student participation, there is usually another 2 hours of preparation and cleanup time required of the leader.

6. MOTIVATION

"How do we keep the interest of the gardeners once everything is planted?"

This is a common question—even experienced educators and gardeners ask it. This manual has over 70 activity ideas for keeping young people enthused and excited once the garden is under way. It's a very important part of a successful project—and perhaps a lot easier than you imagined. Just flip through our activity section to see what we mean.

Here are a few additional thoughts on the subject from program leaders:

From Will Zwink, 4-H Community Garden, Albany, N.Y. ..."We used a lot of 4-H and Cooperative Extension pamphlets on gardening for the children. We let the children actively engage in each phase—fertilizing, raking, planting, spreading hay, weeding, harvesting, etc.

"We provided tools and hoses so that all the children would have something to occupy them at the same time. We organized a pumpkin-sunflower contest for the largest one and we opened the garden to entrance eligibility at the Altamont Fair.

"We also got plenty of media coverage so that children could see their faces in the newspaper."

From Carol Coffey, Future Gardeners of Glenn County, Orland, California..."Keep their first garden small or they will be overwhelmed with work and lose interest. A 6-foot by 6-foot plot with four or five varieties of vegetables and flowers planted close together discourages weeds and provides plenty of fresh produce.

"Prepare snacks and many games related to vegetables, flowers, insects and gardening. Youngsters feel excited and proud when they show-and-tell at a project tour. Take pictures of each participant in their garden. Let the children decide on most activities."

Intergenerational Summer Club Tends Garden

In Montpelier, Vermont, there is one group that has no trouble maintaining its school garden throughout the summer. The Lettuce Eat Garden Group is an intergenerational group consisting of students, teachers, senior citizens and other community members initiated to address hunger and local food production. In addition to its many other activities, the group maintains the school garden at the Main Street School during the summer.

One day each week, the group's youngsters take garden produce down to the local farmers' market where, as school garden consultant Joseph Kiefer notes, they easily disarm their customers. The kids have taken on the responsibility of harvesting, setting up and selling vegetables at market without the assistance of adult leaders. Other summer garden group activities include bringing garden produce to the local senior center and to the emergency food shelf.

RON LINEK—MEDINA SUN SENTINEL

"At Rancho Vejar we give our t-shirt awards at the *third* week to denote the contractual arrangement wherein students agree to stick with the program for all 12 weeks."

John Smith
Director of Rancho Vejar
Santa Barbara, California

From Sandra Nadeau, 4-H Gardening, Van Buren, Maine..."In keeping their interest level high, every week when we meet I prepare different activities such as games, crossword puzzles, wordfind and placing the garden steps in order. The children have fun and learn more about gardening and different terms at the same time."

Tips for gardening with youngsters and keeping their interest high

1. Start gardening with children when they are young and curious. Even programs with pre-schoolers have success and fun growing vegetables.

2. Young children can tire easily mentally and physically. When introducing young people to the garden, don't overwhelm them with things to do. Take breaks for other activities.

3. Make the gardening experience fun. Too many youngsters see gardening as a chore; give them the total gardening experience, not just specific, repetitive tasks.

4. Clearly define what's expected of youngsters before asking them to commit themselves. Be clear about the work and time required, what the harvest could be and also the fun they can have.

5. When explaining garden techniques and information, use visual aids: charts, slides, skits (with gardeners participating), field guides, plant and insect collections.

6. Encourage questions and help people find the answers.

7. Don't impose your expectations on the gardeners. Kids don't care too much about total yields. The experience of growing is as important as the end product. A single radish is cherished by the child if she grew it herself.

8. Involve the children in much of the decision-making (what to plant, where to plant, etc.) so that it becomes 'their' garden. This can be very empowering and will encourage feelings of ownership which will foster interest, motivation and creativity.

9. For very young children, you may want to use a standard garden plan so instructions are the same for all and planting time won't be hectic. Allow room in each plan for at least one vegetable and one flower of the youngster's choice. Grow plants that are quick to mature.

10. Put a limit on planting. Children are usually most excited about planting and harvesting. Instead of planting more than they can take care of, switch to other activities. Taking care of the garden later won't be overwhelming.

11. Start small. It's important that each young person have his or her own garden space, but it doesn't have to be a large one.

12. Plant crops and varieties that are hardy and likely to be successful in your area. Some experimentation is fine, but you do want to insure a measure of success.

13. Meet with gardeners on a regular schedule. Twice a week may be best, with one or two hours for each session.

14. Don't assume youngsters understand gardening concepts that you haven't fully explained or demonstrated. Your notion of planting, thinning or cultivating may be quite different from a young person's

idea. Take the time to explain and demonstrate your terms and techniques.

15. One of the big reasons youngsters garden is to eat food they've grown. Have salad parties, make a class cookbook and test your recipes.

16. Capitalize on children's desire to share what they know with others. When young people want to be helpful, let them.

17. If space permits, think about bringing animals into the project. No matter how exciting plants are to kids, animals are even more exciting. Learning about chickens, rabbits, cows and bees goes along with a garden project.

18. There are many right ways to garden, and the garden is one place where everyone can succeed. Encourage individuality.

19. Don't treat dead or diseased plants as failures. Treat them as interesting opportunities to learn about plant needs, insects, and weather in a positive light.

20. Connect your gardening program to the larger community by planning field trips to food, farm and garden-related places (nursery, orchard, food pantry, apiary, dairy, etc.).

FRIENDS OF THE HARVEST

GRANT HEILMAN

Plan some time tending animals, if possible, to keep kids' interest high.

2

PLANNING FOR SUCCESS

"I've come to realize that the key to success with a gardening program for children is organization. It really helps to map out the garden on paper and to have all necessary materials on hand before attempting to garden with 25 or 30 youngsters. One doesn't have to be a teacher to imagine the chaos that can ensue if children are allowed to plant a sizeable garden with little or no direction."

Bob Peak, Teacher
Plaza Park School
Evansville, Indiana

CHECKLIST FOR A SUCCESSFUL YOUTH GARDEN

Whether your project is small or large, lasts a week or a year, here are some important points to consider.

Write a program plan early

Many months before starting, you should write a program plan for your own use, and to share. Try to include the answers to these questions:

Why are you starting a youth garden program?
Who will participate and how long will it last?
What are the objectives?
What tools and supplies will you need?
What will the kids do once they're involved?
How much will it cost and what are your funding possibilities?
Do you have the support of your school or organization administration?

Although your plan may change many times before the program is actually underway, this outline is an important guide. An early and wholehearted investment in this organizational tool will save time and energy in the long run.

Line up the participants

Most people starting a youth garden program have a possible group of participants already in mind because they are working with kids in some way.

But there are some avid gardeners who love to work with children and want to start a program but don't know how to recruit kids. Putting a classified ad in the local newspaper has worked for some; advertising in the school system is another way. Perhaps easier is to link up with a youth-serving group, a YMCA, for example, to reach the same kids. Linking with another group has several advantages:

• You immediately have an existing organizational framework, with a communications network, possible land, youth leaders, children, a budget, and scheduled times for youth activities.

• It adds credibility if you are trying to raise money for your garden program.

• It enriches and strengthens the existing program by adding a gardening segment.

Ted Unkles of LISTEN, Inc., in New Hampshire started a youth garden program by linking with a local 4-H group. There were only girls in the 4-H club and Ted wanted boys to be in the garden as well. So what did he do? "I told all the girls to challenge the boys at school in a contest to see who could grow the best gardens. Sure enough, we had several boys sign up for the program," he said.

Administrative Support is Critical

If you are a schoolteacher embarking on a gardening project, it's extremely important to secure the support of school administrators at every stage of the process. Your principal's support is key to the sustained success of the program and can be integral to engaging the support of other school administrators. In addition to the basic garden program design, be sure to discuss such issues as curriculum, appropriateness of the site, liability coverage. Not to be forgotten is the janitorial staff. Custodians can greatly help or hinder your gardening efforts. Ask their advice regarding such issues as use of water systems, electrical considerations (if using indoor lights) and tool storage.

WANTED: Kids ages 8-12 interested in participating in a youth garden program. Learn how to grow your own food. Have fun doing special activities in and around the garden. Call Fred and Sally for details 222-1111.

WASHINGTON. EATONVILLE DISPATCH

Other ways to recruit gardeners:

*Put up posters inviting the kids to sign up.

*Show slides on the garden program, giving them a better idea of what's involved. It's important to make it clear from the beginning what is to be expected of them, and what they can expect from the garden program. Some 4-H leaders have a two-page contract which sets goals for the young gardener and checkpoints for his or her progress.

*Show slides of harvest parties, craft projects, picnics and field trips as well as kids gardening.

*Schedule introductory activities for gardeners. Kids like making veggie creatures or popping home-grown popcorn.

Find good land for garden site

You can garden almost anywhere but some sources of land to consider are:

- community gardens
- school grounds and city parks
- home of parents of participants
- churches
- corporations
- vacant lots
- nature centers
- retirement centers
- residential institutions

Locating a site and getting permission to use it can be a long process, so allow plenty of time. Also, the site you pick will need to be prepared for gardens, if it is not already under cultivation.

Plan special activities

As early as possible, develop a solid activity program. It's not something which should wait until the youngsters arrive at the site. Post the schedule of activities in an area where the kids can find it. Seeing the plan will encourage them to join the project, and more importantly, it will keep their interest once the program is underway.

With a plan, you'll have time to get supplies and try out activities before doing them with the kids. A primary reason children's garden projects fail is because the kids lose interest; they are bored. For the sake of the youngsters, make the most of their time, and yours, by integrating special activities into the program.

Decide whether to grow your own transplants

Many vegetables grown in school or youth gardens are planted as transplants. Transplants are used when the time required for a crop to reach maturity is longer than the growing season for an area, such as tomatoes grown in Michigan; or to obtain an early harvest, such as setting onion plants to get early scallions.

Vegetable transplants may appear expensive at the local retail garden store. Before deciding to grow your own, however, consider the following advantages and disadvantages of doing it yourself.

ADVANTAGES
1. It's a learning experience.
2. There's a greater choice of varieties to try.
3. Growing your own might be cheaper, if you grow a lot! (Note: Keep in mind that many locally owned garden centers will sell transplants to schools at reduced prices.)
4. Less root-bound stock.

DISADVANTAGES
1. Start-up materials are costly, (flats, cell paks, growing medium, fertilizer, lights, etc.)
2. Large amount of space required with temperature of 70-75° F. days, 60-65° F. nights.
3. Greenhouse, south windows or supplemental grow lights required. Many make the mistake of growing plants with insufficient light (for example, near north windows).
4. Much time (including weekends) involved in care, particularly for watering.
5. Careful scheduling is necessary to insure transplants of correct size for planting dates.
6. Potential growing problems, (insects, damping off and seed rot diseases).
7. Plants must be hardened off properly before planting.

SOURCE: Project ROOTS
Title IV-C
Michigan State Dept. of Education
Lansing School District
Lansing, Michigan

KENT BADGER—PITTSBURGH PRESS

Growing seedlings indoors at junior high school at Apollo, Pennsylvania

Gardening know-how

As stated before, if *you* don't have it, it's not the end of the world, but make sure someone working very closely with you and your program knows gardening.

Not knowing how to garden and not having confidence in your gardening capabilities are two different things. We've learned that people who want to start youth gardening programs are usually experienced gardeners who want to share the joys of gardening with young people. But many of these people are not confident about taking responsibility for the success of the children's gardens.

One leader told us, "One of the most fulfilling aspects of my own work with the youth gardening programs is preparing for our weekly lessons and activities. It gives me a chance to research gardening questions that I never would have taken the time to do for my own home garden. I began to question why you do this and that. I became a better gardener and I think my own enthusiasm and desire to know more had a positive impact on the kids."

FRIENDS OF THE HARVEST

Tools and supplies

An initial investment in durable tools of good quality is a good idea since children are particularly hard on them.

Given the choice between standard, adult-sized tools, and smaller, floral-sized tools, children will first go for the larger tools. But eventually they turn to smaller tools, especially short-handled tools, since these are easier to work with.

Regardless of size, providing the "real thing" is important. Toy tools make gardening tasks more difficult and are frustrating to use.

Below are the basic tools that you will likely want to acquire:

• **Shovels**—important for digging, turning, scooping. While round, pointed shovels are best for hard ground, square spades are nice for making clean edges on beds.

• **Spading forks**—have sturdy, flat prongs that are excellent for such activities as breaking up clods of soil, working in organic matter, moving compost, digging potatoes.

• **Rakes**—used for breaking smaller clods, leveling beds, spreading soil and organic materials.

• **Hoes**—used for making furrows, cultivating, weeding.

• **Hand trowels**—important tools for transplanting seedlings.

• **Hand cultivators**—used for weeding and cultivating around growing plants.

• **Wheelbarrow or cart**—helpful for moving soil, compost, manure, other materials.

• **Watering devices**—these might include watering cans, hoses with attachments and sprinklers.

• **Other materials**—consider your need for stakes, string, measuring tape, harvest knives and signs.

Getting insurance is usually a routine matter

We've yet to hear from any youth gardening groups about serious injury occurring on a site, but accidents can happen. Be sure both your group and the landowner have proper insurance protection against property damage or personal injury claims.

If the youth gardens are located on school grounds, they are probably covered under the school's basic liability insurance. Check with the administration because the insurance carrier may have to be notified when a garden is started.

Municipal, county, state, or federal lands should already have public liability insurance. Make sure your activity is covered under the policy.

If you are gardening on private land, the landowner may insist that you carry liability insurance. The school, 4-H club, botanical garden, or other sponsoring group can usually attach a rider to its existing liability policy for coverage at little or no cost.

6 ft. 3 in.

3 ft

2 ft

2 ft

6 ft.

A durable, easy-to-build tool locker.

FOR YEAR-ROUND SCHOOL GARDENS, A GOOD CALENDAR HELPS!

Garden calendars from around the country

The following are sample garden calendars for planning a school garden year in several regions of the country. These are based on actual calendars designed by garden leaders. Remember that there are endless indoor and outdoor garden-based activities that can be tied into the curriculum throughout the year to supplement these basic outlines.

South

July, August

Soil tests; till gardens (no plowing); add manure and rotted leaves; get seeds.

September

Talk with teachers during first week of school to work out schedules; tool and garden safety; vegetable selections by students; plant, weed and thin; transplant; start growth charts; discuss plant parts and their functions.

October

Assistant county agent for horticulture talks to students; transplant; start compost pile (show film); talk about home gardens; weed and thin; fertilize with fish emulsion.

November

Discuss plant nutrients (test); study plant pests; human nutrition (reports by students in upper grades); nutrition specialist talks to students; begin harvesting early crops; plant parsley for Christmas presents.

December

Harvest; student evaluation of gardening program.

January

No classes. Prepare beds for spring gardens; add manure and leaf mold; till beds, take inventory of seeds; work out spring schedule.

February

Garden and tool safety; plant nutrients (test); plant pests; human nutrition and health (reports); nutrition specialist talks to students; students select vegetables to plant; plant early crops in late February; start growth charts; plant parts and functions.

March

Plant vegetables; composting; soil and water conservation and pollution; thin, weed, transplant.

April

Assistant county agent talks to students; weed; study plant pests; fertilize; harvest; discuss home gardens.

May

Harvest; discuss attitudes and values, especially regarding gardening; benefits of gardening.

June

No school gardens.

New England

September

Do site planning; test soil; stake out gardens; plant green manure crop; begin compost pile. Prepare site for strawberry planting next spring. Outside speaker to visit and help with the above. Request PTO funding for tools and storage; write letter to parents explaining project and asking for gifts of extra tools, time, etc.

October

Field trips: local farm museum to study colonial tools, farming and farm life; historic farm tour; trip to cider mill. Walk in woods and collect wildflower seeds for bird feeders. Turn and add compost.

November

Filmstrips on nutrition. Nutrition curriculum activities. Start houseplant cuttings for Christmas.

December

Prepare for seed ordering; get catalogs; letter to parents for seed funding and donations.

January

Seed ordering. Study germination, basic plant growth needs. Plan and build coldframes.

February

Divide the seeds and distribute; university speaker—"Plants are Like People." Plan and draw garden maps.

March

Start seedlings; group lesson with demonstration; start charts of seedling growth.

April

Prepare soil; plow under cover crop; add compost; dig beds; plant early crops. Plant strawberry plants.

May

Transplanting, thinning, mulching, weeding seedlings; garden experiments; class projects; start garden journals; school beautification.

June

Early harvesting; set up summer gardening schedule (to be sent home with definitive days for the children to help); plan fall harvest festival which will include: a garden feast; exhibits of vegetables; garden art and written work; activities such as grinding corn, making vegetable prints, making flour, carrot juice, cider; demonstrations of sheep shearing.

West

September

Students return to harvest potatoes, cantaloupes and popcorn planted previous spring; work on soil preparation for winter garden.

October

Plant winter garden of radishes, broccoli, carrots, cabbage, turnips and other cool weather crops; harvest olives, cure and can them; harvest pumpkins and celebrate fall harvest. Bring food to local food pantry and senior citizen's center.

November

Weed and maintain winter garden; prepare rows for strawberry planting; cover strawberry mounds with plastic and cut slits for plants; set in 12,000 berry plants.

December

Clean and weed orchard area (125 fruit trees). Ongoing indoor garden-based experiments and activities.

January

Prune fruit trees; paint picnic tables and swings. Have a midwinter salad party with cool weather vegetables.

February

Prune one-year-old grape plants to one cane; set posts and wires for new plants; fertilize berry plants.

March

Begin strawberry harvest; start indoor seedlings of vegetables and flowers; plow under winter garden residues; prepare soil for spring plantings.

April

Plant spring garden with early crops; harvest more strawberries.

May

Care for and weed spring gardens; pick even more strawberries for strawberry festival; side-dress early crops; watch for bugs; keep records.

June

Spring harvest fair. Send produce home with children, plan for special summer activities.

July-August

Adults tend community gardens and children help out on occasion.

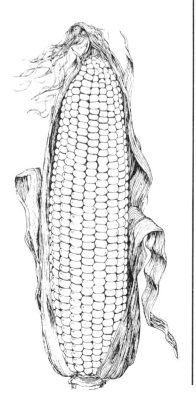

MARK HEBERT

Year-round Indoor Garden Plan

This calendar can be used in any geographic area since it relies on raising a garden indoors, under lights. See chapter 6 for more on indoor gardening.

September
Class assembly of indoor growing unit. Seed ordering; letters to seed companies; start houseplant cuttings for Thanksgiving gifts.

October
Study and experiment with germination, photosynthesis, soils; build root-view boxes. Sow long-season crops for winter salad party. Make sprouts for tasting. World Food Day activities.

November
Start growth charts and records. Begin variety trials and fertilizer experiments. Bring home houseplant gifts.

December
Sow more seeds for salad party. Study and begin activities relating to composting. Build worm boxes and start 'worm farm.'

January
Start marigold seeds for Mother's Day flowering plant gifts. Study insects and diseases. Determine seedling needs for outdoor garden.

February
Study pollination and hand pollinate cucumbers. Valentine's Day salad harvest party. Start early seedlings for garden.

March
Start seedlings for outdoor garden and spring plant sale. Field trip to hydroponic greenhouse.

April
Transplant seedlings; move some out to coldframes. Start nutrition unit.

May
Spring plant sale; bring home Mother's Day flowers. Move remainder of seedlings to outdoor garden.

June
Clean and disassemble indoor growing unit. Sterilize containers.

CLEVELAND PUBLIC SCHOOLS

Gardening lessons continue all year long!

Here's one teacher's vision of how a garden project can send youngsters on the path toward almost any subject. Developed by teacher Vicki Greenhouse for her second and third grade students in Lincoln, Vermont.

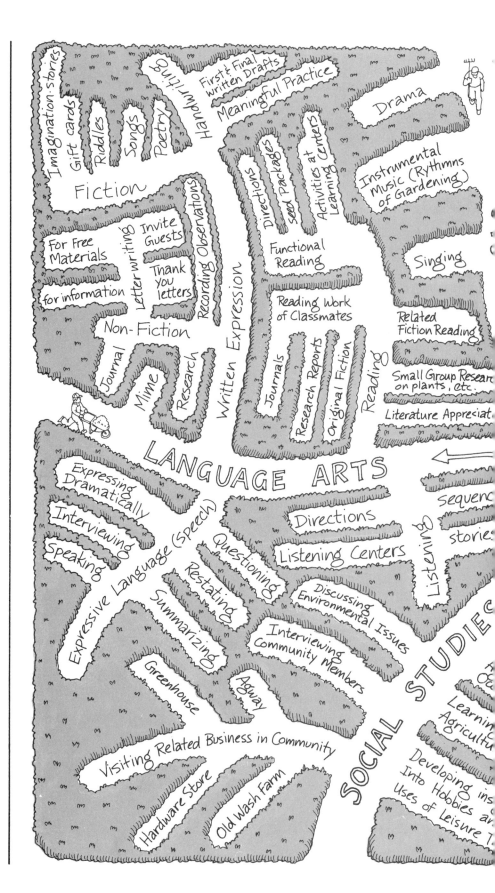

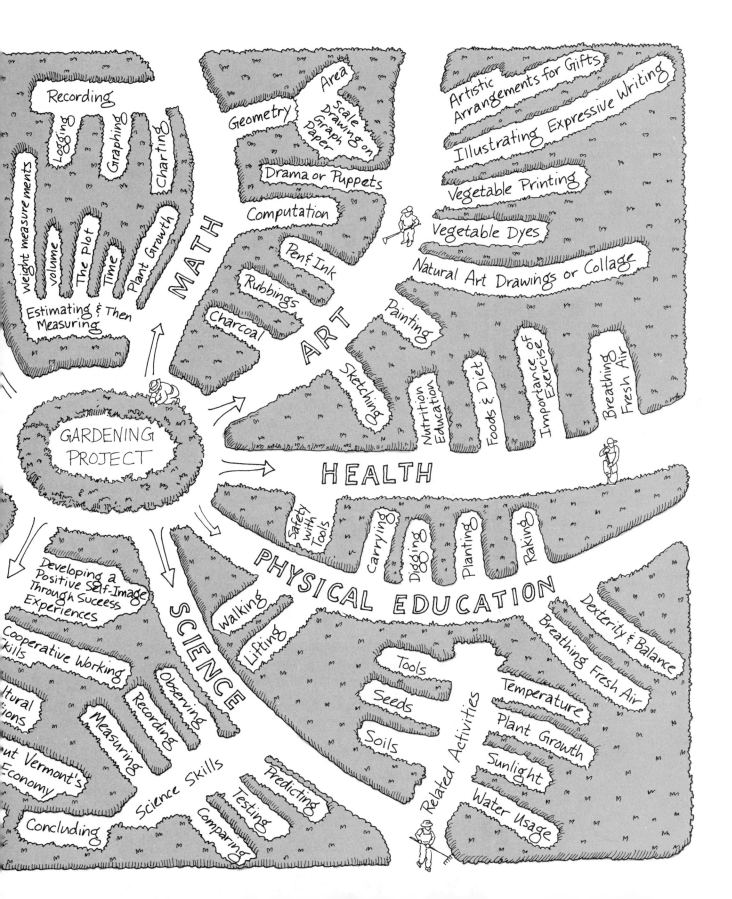

28

PLAN A HARVEST PARTY TO CLOSE OUT THE PROGRAM!

A harvest party is a time to share in the rewards of a garden, to recognize the accomplishments of the gardeners and to thank people who've helped out. It's also a time to have fun. Here are some planning pointers:

Potluck cookout or supper

Ask guests to bring a dish to share and encourage them to use fresh garden produce.

Award ceremony

Every youngster should receive an award, if possible. Cite outstanding accomplishments, too, such as "best potato beetle picker-offer!"

Hail the helpers

A certificate of appreciation is a good way to express your thanks to people who've contributed to your program. Invite a public figure to help with the presentations.

Plan for games

You don't need much equipment or athletic skills to have fun. Include non-competitive games so everyone can be a winner.

Displays and exhibits

This gives children the chance to display their achievements. Besides produce, invite exhibits of garden crafts, flower arrangements or essays.

Slide show

Kids as well as adults love to see themselves on screen. Start early in the season and collect slides of everyday and special events.

A last harvest

If there's harvesting to be done, there's no better time than when the gang's all assembled.

Fund-raising

Possible winners: garden craft sale, pumpkin carving contest with entry fee, dinner and dance for adults, auction of donated gifts.

Work party

A harvest party may be the right time to ask for help in building a fence or putting in a new water system.

Guest log

Keep a record of the people who come to the party. It'll help in fund-raising or in getting the project under way next season.

Fun Group Activities

There are two good books available from The New Games Foundation which give instructions for group games that involve people of all ages. *The New Games Book*, edited by Andrew Fluegelman and *More New Games* by Andrew Fluegelman, cost $7.95 each. They can be ordered from The New Games Foundation, P.O. Box 7901, San Francisco, CA 94130 or found at your local bookstore.

Lettuce Eat Garden Group, Montpelier, VT.

Share Your Harvest

In addition to sharing with families and friends, harvest time can be a good focus for raising awareness about local hunger issues. Encourage the students to find out about local food relief organizations (food pantry, soup kitchen, etc.) and make plans for donating some produce to these groups. Organizations for the home-bound, the elderly and local community action programs can be contacted for information regarding food donations.

And don't forget your sponsors! You might show your appreciation for their support by creating a 'thank-you' harvest basket. Part of the fun of gardening comes with being able to show off and share the fruits of one's labor.

CHAPTER

3

DEVELOPING YOUR SITE

"These children are our country's future, and so is our farmland. We want to teach them to love the soil and how to keep it fertile and the joy of seeing things grow."

Louise Bastable,
Community Gardener
North Shore Community Gardens
Middleton, Massachusetts

Here is some solid information on the technical aspects of a good youth garden project...choosing a garden site, improving soils, designing the layout of your garden site, and how to get basic gardening chores, such as liming, fertilizing and watering done on a large site.

Here and there, what we cover may seem too basic for experienced garden organizers, but the information is vital to those new in the field. We believe there are also plenty of new ideas for the long-time youth gardening advocate.

CHOOSING THE RIGHT SITE

Sometimes only one piece of land is available for your project and you have to take it or leave it. But if you have several alternatives, being selective at the beginning can save you headaches later. There's a lot to look for in a large garden site.

So, examine very carefully the field or vacant area you are considering. Good agricultural land is ideal, but most any site with at least 6 inches of topsoil is a good potential garden area. The presence of sod or a good crop of weeds usually means garden vegetables will do well. We strongly advise taking a soil sample to test for nutrients and the pH level of the soil. Identifying the soil type (clay, sand, silt or combination) will also help you evaluate its suitability.

Try to avoid sites that are exposed to pollutants from major highways, industry smokestacks, and airports. Even recent agricultural soils might contain residues from herbicides which inhibit vegetable growth for a season or two.

An important site consideration—is the soil contaminated with lead?

Urban gardeners should be very cautious in choosing a garden site because some city soils are contaminated with lead from lead-based paints and auto exhaust. If your potential garden site had houses or other painted structures on it, or if it is close to a heavily-travelled road, there may be dangerous levels of lead in the soil. Lead does not break down, nor does it leach out of the soil.

You may also suspect lead contamination if the garden site was once used for waste dumping, or if it was an orchard. Fruit trees were treated with lead arsenate insecticide beginning in the 1890's and continuing until the 1950's. The lead residues from the insecticide remain in the soils today.

Lead pollution can present a health hazard to all gardeners, but young children are most affected by it. Lead causes anemia and harms the kidneys and brain.

Children with continuous exposure to low levels of lead may show no apparent early symptoms, but can suffer irreversible damage. Pregnant women and nursing mothers should know that lead can harm the developing child by crossing the placenta and also by passing to an infant through breast milk.

If you suspect the presence of lead in your soils, have the soil tested. Call your local Extension Service, your state Department of Agriculture, or your Public Health Department to find out where lead testing of soils is available.

If your soil does have unacceptable levels of lead for youth gardening activities, seek alternatives:

*Choose another site with low lead levels;

*Grow container gardens, using clean topsoil;

*Prepare raised beds, line them with plastic, fill with clean topsoil or soil-less mix, and plant. Mulch around the beds or plant a ground cover to protect soil;

*Or replenish your garden soil with clean topsoil. (You'll need professional help with this big job. Consult your Extension Service.)

If your garden is within 50 feet of a heavily travelled street, you can cut lead contamination from auto exhaust:

*Plant a hedge or build a fence to keep automobile exhaust out.

*Do not plant leafy greens (spinach, beet tops, loose leaf lettuce, herbs, turnip greens, etc.) because it is impossible to wash all the lead from their soft porous surfaces.

*Wash all produce thoroughly.

*Discard older, outer leaves of vegetables, such as cabbage, before eating.

*Mulch to keep airborne lead off the soil surface so that it can't wash down into the soil. Do not use organic mulches for this purpose because they will end up incorporated into the garden soil.

For further reading on the subject, write for the free booklet "Lead in the Soil, A Gardener's Handbook," available from the Suffolk County Extension Service, University of Massachusetts, Downtown Center, Room 908, Boston, MA 02125.

Slope—less is better

Gardens should be laid out on reasonably level ground. Avoid steep slopes—they are generally less fertile and gardens can be damaged by water runoff and soil erosion. If the site has greater than a 20-degree slope, some sort of terracing or raised beds will usually be necessary.

Look for good drainage

Good soil drainage is necessary for good plant growth. Most vegetables will not grow well in saturated, muddy soils. A soil with good crumbly texture will usually drain well. Check to see if there is much puddling after a hard rain, or if there's any possibility of flooding.

Heavy soils which don't drain well may be okay for experienced gardeners, but in a youth garden where teaching and demonstrations are important, heavy soils will limit the number of days you can be in the garden with kids.

A little shade is fine

The site should be in an open location exposed to full sunlight for at least 6 hours a day. A southern exposure with very little shading from trees or buildings is ideal. Check the site at different times during the day to see how much sun it receives. Use shady areas for play or rest areas, or for some shade-tolerant crops, such as greens and cabbage.

Existing vegetation and fixtures may help

Trees, hedges, buildings or fences on the north or west side of the garden will provide protection from strong prevailing winds and stormy weather. Wildflowers, shrubs, or rock outcroppings can be attractively incorporated into your site design with a little forethought.

Small buildings or old foundations can be renovated into tool storage areas or garden work areas. Fences or buildings to the north, east, or west can be used as borders and protection from intruders.

Is the site big enough?

Is there room enough for all your planned activities and future expansion? The first thing is to determine how many gardeners you'll have and how big the garden plots will be. Your project might require pathways, truck access and land for cold frames, compost, tool storage sheds and parking. Jot down all the activities you'd like to see at the site and sketch a draft design of the site. This will help you compare potential sites.

Gardeners should be able to enter and leave the garden easily without hazards. Access by bikes, cars, and public transportation routes is important.

Water source is essential

Access to water is essential for garden sites in most areas of the country, and the closer water is to the gardens the better. We've seen lots of different watering arrangements at group gardens. They include:

*Neighboring houses or buildings with outdoor faucets whose owners are willing to let you hook up a temporary line.

*Nearby fire hydrants tapped with permission from the local fire or water department.

*Tapping in on existing underground municipal lines running near the site. (A metered line is often installed.)

Special adaptors needed to connect garden hose to standard fire hydrant.

*Pumping from nearby streams, ponds, or lakes with hand pumps. (If you're in an industrial area, test water for harmful pollutants.)

*A well point can be driven to draw water up where underground water levels are near the surface.

*Asking fire departments to fill up used storage tanks or 55-gallon steel drums periodically during the season.

Look to the future

One of the most important questions when deciding upon a site is, how long can our group use this site? Just one year, two, ten, how many? Does the landowner or school department have plans for development or other use of the property?

Many good gardening programs have lost sites because of short-term or non-binding agreements with landowners.

Most groups use land on a year-to-year basis; a few have written leases, others verbal agreements. For your own protection and future security, find a site you can grow on for a long time.

SPRUCING UP THE SITE

You may have to clear out trash and other debris from you site before you do anything else. The job usually goes faster—and is a lot more fun—if you can get a gang of youngsters to help.

Have some tools and a supply of heavy-duty garbage bags or cartons on hand. For lots of rubbish, try to get a commercial dumpster for a weekend to chuck rubble into. Check with the sanitation company, public works department or a construction firm to borrow one. Some of the junk might be useful—bricks, concrete blocks, and lumber can be used to make planting beds, fences, or paths.

Some sites require big equipment for clearing and grading. Your city street, highway, or public works department, or even the National Guard, might help with heavy site work. Construction firms or general contractors might be willing to contribute some help. A bulldozer can scrape away trees and rubble and grade the site. Backhoes can dig deep for stumps or foundations and lift heavy items into a dump truck to be hauled away. Fees for site work range from $30-$75 per hour. Before turning big equipment loose on your site, though, inquire about any underground utility lines or water and sewage pipes. Also, ask for design help from a local landscape architect before shaping the lot.

Hard-working youngsters in Holyoke, Massachusetts.

VINCENT S. D'ADDARIO

TIPS ON SOIL TESTING

Chemical soil testing determines the amount of major nutrients in the soil and its level of acidity (pH). These tests can be run at the Extension Service or state agricultural experiment station, usually for a small fee. Results will usually include recommendations for problems shown by the tests.

An alternative to laboratory tests is a do-it-yourself soil test kit with chemical solutions to test for major nutrients and pH levels. Tests in some kits are complicated, so they wouldn't make good projects for young children.

A good kit has instructions for analyzing the tests and recommendations for fertilizing. Results are not exact but they do provide a range of high and lows. They are helpful for spot checks throughout the season.

Fall is the best time to test soils because you have time to begin treating the land for next season's use. Test when soils are dry. If you test in the early spring, wait until the soil has warmed up. Do not test immediately after adding organic matter or soil amendments.

Use a trowel, a sampling probe, or a spade to gather a sample of soil from a depth of 6 inches. Take several samples from across the site. It is best to take a sample from each corner of the site and several in the center to get a true representation of the soil.

A handy reference

Incorrect pH levels should be adjusted before gardening at your site. If the pH is too low, ground limestone or wood ashes are used to raise it; if the pH is too high, sulphur is used to lower it.

TO RAISE ONE UNIT OF pH (BASED ON 100 SQ. FT.)			
	Hydrated lime	Dolomitic or Ground	Wood ashes
Light soils	3 lbs.	5 lbs.	5 lbs.
Heavy soils	6 lbs.	10-12 lbs.	7 lbs.

TO LOWER SOIL ONE UNIT OF pH (BASED ON 100 SQ. FT.)	
	Sulphur
Light soils	1 lb.
Heavy soils	2 lbs.

Do you need extra topsoil?

If you don't have 6-12 inches of topsoil on your site, you'll need to bring in more by truck. (A raised bed growing system will help conserve soil and organic matter and might be an alternative to importing topsoil.)

Topsoil is expensive, but occasionally you can get it cheap. For instance, you might arrange for soil being cleared from a construction site to be moved to your site. When purchasing topsoil, get it in bulk. The price, at this writing, is in the range of $8-$15 per cubic yard. Dump trucks usually deliver in 7-or 9-cubic yard loads. Inquire if the topsoil is screened or

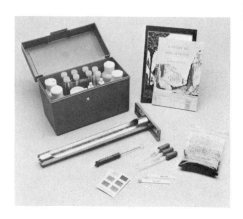

Some other soil testing and liming tips:

- **Do not touch samplings with your hands.**
- **Mix samples in a clean container or paper bag.**
- **Remove solids such as stones or debris.**
- **Take a sampling from this mixture for your test (a full baggie is adequate). If testing several sites, be sure to label your bags carefully.**
- **If the property has decidedly different soil types, take separate samples.**
- **Test every two to three years or when you detect a nutrient deficiency problem.**
- **One application of lime or sulphur is usually effective for two to four years. Fall application is best. If liming in spring, work lime into the soil a few inches before planting.**
- **If you need to change pH more than one unit, make the changes gradually. Add lime each season until you reach the desired level.**
- **Don't apply more than 40 lbs. per 1,000 sq. ft. in one year.**
- **Heavy soils require large amounts of lime because they have a larger storage capacity.**
- **Be conservative in your use of limestone. It's easier to raise pH than to lower it.**
- **Hydrated lime works almost immediately. Other lime sources are best applied in the fall for the following season.**
- **Frequent additions of well-decomposed organic matter will help stabilize correct pH levels.**
- **To lime a large site, hire a lime company with a spreader truck.**

unscreened (screened is better for gardens) and where it comes from. If you're buying a lot from one source, take a soil test to get an idea of the topsoil's general value.

Topsoil formula

To figure out how much topsoil to buy, determine the area of the garden (in square feet) and the depth of the soil required.

Use this formula to figure out how many cubic yards of soil you'll need:

Length of site (in feet) × width (in feet) × depth to be covered (in feet) = this will equal the cubic feet needed. To convert to cubic yards, divide the number by 27.

Example: for a 50-foot by 25-foot area

My Garden is: 50ft × 25ft
I want 12" of topsoil (1 ft.)

So: (L×W) × depth of topsoil = cubic feet needed.

Or: 50' × 25' × 1' = 1250 cubic feet

Now: I divide cu. ft. by 27 = cubic yards

1250 ÷ 27 = 46 cubic yards topsoil

needed for 12" deep

If: I only want 6" topsoil;

50' × 25' × .5' = 625 ÷ 27 = 23 cu. yds

Or: For 3" topsoil;

50' × 25' × .25' = 312.5 ÷ 27 = 12 cu. yds.

A good rule of thumb: one cubic yard will cover 54 square feet with 6 inches of top soil.

When the topsoil is delivered, be at the site to make sure it's unloaded in the right place. If spreading by hand, dump it in a central area so it's easier to cover the garden. Sometimes the driver can back the truck in and pull out slowly to spread topsoil across the site.

TURN OVER YOUR LAND EARLY

Your garden land must be opened up early to get rid of weeds and grasses and to start getting the soil in condition. This turning can be done by hand, by a small roto-tiller, or by a farm-size tractor with plowing attachments.

At least two turnings are recommended—several weeks before planting season, and then once again right before planting day. More frequent tillings will speed up the job of getting weeds under control and conditioning the field. Working the ground early leaves time for organic matter and plowed-under grass and roots to decompose.

If you've got energy and time and your garden area is small, you might prepare the garden area with hand tools. That gets people involved and creates an important connection between gardener and the soil, but it can exhaust and discourage youngsters who are not up to the task.

Roto-tillers

Small engine roto-tillers do a good job in preparing new gardens. Some youth projects even own their own machines. (Denver's Cunningham Elementary School had a fund-raising drive to purchase theirs.) The use of roto-tillers is limited to areas up to an acre or so. If your plot is bigger, it pays to use larger equipment.

Roto-tillers have many uses—turning over new ground, mixing in organic matter and fertilizers, cultivating, preparing seed beds, and tilling under crop residues in the fall. Tilling a new area is hard work and will take several hours, depending on soil type and area.

Having access to a roto-tiller during the season is helpful. You can use it to plow under weedy areas, turn under crop residues after early harvests, and keep the site looking neat and clean. (A ship-shape garden is impressive—when you give someone a tour you won't be embarrassed.)

Getting to know tractors

Small tractors the size of riding lawnmowers often have plowing or roto-tilling attachments for working up a new garden site. They can be rented or hired out in most areas. More common for sites an acre or larger is farm-size equipment, 18-horsepower tractors and larger. The bigger tractors handle most jobs better, faster, and at lower cost than the small riding machines.

A plow on new ground will dig down 6 to 12 inches and spill over the earth, leaving large chunks of sod bottom-side up. Let the soil sit for several weeks if possible to allow grass and weeds to die out. A second pass is then made with a harrow or disc which will slice the big chunks of soil and mix the soil. (If possible, have soil amendments such as lime and manure spread early so they can be worked into the soil.)

Some tractors can pull a *rotovator* attachment, which is basically a large roto-tiller. It is excellent for preparing ground that has already been plowed. Rotovators can also be used for breaking new ground if the soil is not too heavy.

Looking for someone to plow?

Check with your Parks Department, Extension Service, local farm supply stores, or garden centers to find people who do "custom plowing." Farmers are busy in the spring so make your arrangements as early as possible. Landscapers and other equipment owners might also be able to do the job. Rates vary in different sections of the country but usually range from $15-$50 per hour.

FERTILIZE REGULARLY

Vegetables are heavy users of plant foods, so gardens require fertilizing and replenishment of soil nutrients each year.

Most youth gardening organizers have experience in fertilizing home gardens and small areas. But larger sites sometimes are a challenge when trying to raise the organic matter content and nutrient levels of the soil.

The soundest method of gardening relies on a constant replenishment of nutrients and minerals derived from organic materials such as manures, rock powders, compost and plant materials such as cover crops, leaves and grass clippings. These fertilizers add organic matter and provide a slow, continued release of nutrients throughout the season.

In case of severe deficiencies, chemical fertilizers will raise the nutrient levels quickly, as long as the pH level is correct. Once immediate deficiencies are corrected, it's best to rely on organic matter and natural fertilizers to keep your site in shape.

Tips for fertilizing

There are several pre-mixed natural fertilizers that are easy to use and provide excellent results. Good brands to look for are Fertrell Super N, Earthrite C, Nitro, or Milorganite. These can be purchased in 50-pound bags or in larger quantities from farm and garden supply centers and applied over a large site with a manual hopper-spreader. The spreader is wheeled over the site and set to spread the fertilizer at the desired rate.

Many group gardening programs choose to condition the entire site the first year to ensure proper nutrient levels and then fertilize individual plots separately each year thereafter. Your park or school department probably has fertilizer spreaders for their tractors that will apply fertilizer evenly over a big area. Local farmers or landscape contractors should be asked for assistance, too.

Dried fertilizers can be spread by hand, too. It takes longer, though. Put desired amounts of fertilizer into buckets or wheelbarrows and spread by hand. Walk slowly down strips of the field and make a semi-circular throw with each step. Choose a calm day for this kind of spreading (a good project with kids).

On a large site, manures (cow, horse, chicken or other) are easily applied by manure spreaders. Local farmers are often willing to lend

LINDA LUTZ

assistance or your parks department might have the necessary equipment. Manure should be spread before your garden is tilled in the spring.

If you can't get power equipment, then use good ol' hand labor. If you get loads of organic material or fertilizers delivered, ask to have several piles distributed around the site for easier spreading.

Converting fertilizer recommendations from "lbs./acre" to "lbs./sq. ft."

RECOMMENDATION

Garden area sq. ft.	100 lbs/acre	400 lbs./acre	2000 lbs./acre
100 sq. ft.	.25 lb. or ½ cup	1 lb. or 2 cups	5 lbs. or 10
500 sq. ft.	1.25 lbs.	5 lbs.	25 lbs.
1000 sq. ft.	2.5 lbs.	10 lbs.	50 lbs.
2000 sq. ft.	5 lbs.	20 lbs.	100 lbs.

Bagged fertilizer weighs approximately one pound to the pint; one pint is equal to 2 cups.

Emphasize natural fertilizers if you can

About the easiest way to fertilize garden plots is by using the handy bagged fertilizer available at garden centers. Most commercial fertilizers are usually chemically synthesized, easy to apply, and quick-acting.

Natural fertilizers, on the other hand, are harder to find, handle, and affect crops more slowly. Still, they offer many opportunities to teach youngsters about our natural resources, the interdependence of people and animals, and about how gardening was done in the good ol' days.

Try to find local sources for natural fertilizers, and use them to teach important lessons. As sources of *nitrogen,* look for chicken, cow, horse, pig or sheep manures; cottonseed meal, blood meal or alfalfa meal. For *phosphorous,* locate bone meal and rock phosphate. For *potassium,* use wood ashes, greensand or granite dust. (For charts on this subject, see *Encylopedia of Organic Gardening,* Rodale Press.)

Side-dressing know-how

"Side-dressings," or second helpings of fertilizer during the growing season, are very important for vegetables growing in new garden soil or in sandy soil lacking organic matter. Timely extra feedings of plant food are essential to good harvests.

To side-dress with chemical fertilizers, add 1-2 tablespoons of 5-10-10 per plant. Dig a shallow furrow around plants or along rows several inches away from plant stems or under the drip line of outer leaves. Be sure to cover the fertilizer with soil to keep it from splashing onto plant leaves.

Good natural side-dressings include a couple of handfuls of compost or dried manure per plant, or a watering with liquid seaweed or fish emulsion.

Side-dressing chart

CROP	WHEN
Green beans	Not necessary
Beet greens	2 weeks after leaves appear
Beets	When tops are 4-5 inches high. Go light on nitrogen which encourages leaf growth
Broccoli	3 weeks after transplanting; go light on nitrogen
Brussels sprouts	3 weeks after transplant; when sprout begin to appear
Cabbage and cauliflower	If your soil was well-fertilized, no need to sidedress
Carrots	3 weeks after plants are well established
Celery	3 weeks after setting out; again 6 weeks later
Sweet corn	3 weeks after planting; when plants are 8-10 inches high; when tassels appear
Cucumbers	When they first begin to run; when blossoms set
Eggplant	3 weeks after setting out plants
Kale	When plants are 6-8 inches high
Lettuce, head	3 weeks after transplant; as heads form
Melons	When they begin to run; a week after blossoms set; again 3 weeks later
Onions	3 weeks after setting out; when tops are 6-8 inches tall; when bulbs start to swell
Peas (English)	No need
Peppers	3 weeks after transplant; after first fruit set
Potato	When plants bloom
Pumpkin	When plants start to run; at blossom set
Radish	No need to sidedress
Spinach	When plants are about one-third grown
Squash, summer	When plants are about 6 inches tall or when they bloom
Squash, winter	When plants start to run; at blossom set
Tomato	2-3 weeks after transplant; before first picking; two weeks after first picking. Go light on nitrogen
Turnips	When plants are about one-third grown

COMPOSTING, A THRILLING EXPERIENCE FOR YOUNGSTERS!

We recommend that you designate a place for a composting project in your site plan. Composting is more than a way to turn organic wastes into a dark, rich, soil-building ingredient. It's a way to impress youngsters and get them excited about what one leader called "the essence of gardening."

We believe every youth garden should have some sort of compost activity—even if it's a small "baggie compost" project.

The point is, there's magic in composting. It's a process which turns "stinky things" into sweet-smelling soil, turns big chunks of organic matter into tiny pieces, and turns colorful vegetable scraps and leftovers into "black gold." And, unlike synthesized fertilizer, you simply can't use too much compost in your garden.

Some gardening leaders succumb completely to compost magic. At first they think compost piles won't actually work, or that they'd stink and wouldn't be proper near a school garden. But after building a good compost pile, and seeing the magic themselves, they become believers.

Compost piles are simple collections of plant and animal materials piled up enough to decompose through a natural heating process and the work of soil micro-organisms. Compost can be made in bins made of wood, pallets, concrete blocks, snow fencing, chicken wire or even in old garbage cans with holes punched out. All bins need openings for air circulation.

A compost area at least 3 feet by 3 feet with a height of 3 feet or so is best. These dimensions allow you to organize enough material to insulate the pile, whose interior temperatures can reach 150°F. The actual size of the pile will depend on how ambitious you and the kids are and the amount of organic waste available.

Materials to use:

Grass clippings, leaves, hair and feathers, all food scraps (but no meat, bones, or fat), manures, crop residues, and essentially anything that was once alive.

Kids can also bring in organic matter from home. Also check with your street or public works department for leaves as many cities have leaf collection projects.

Building a compost cake

Start by loosening the soil where the pile will sit, to provide good drainage.

A compost cake consists of three layers. Start with a layer of dry materials on the bottom about 4-8 inches deep. Chop large materials before adding them and they'll decompose faster.

Next add a 4-8 inch layer of green vegetation and kitchen wastes. On top of kitchen wastes, add a third layer of soil, but only about 1 inch or so deep.

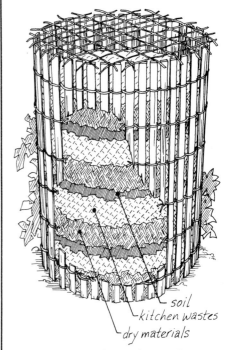

soil
kitchen wastes
dry materials

Proper layering makes good compost.

42

The decomposition process uses up nutrients, especially nitrogen. To speed up the process add nitrogen-rich materials such as bloodmeal, fish meal, cottonseed meal or fresh manure. Two pounds of meal are enough for a big compost pile.

Keep layering until you have a pile about 3 feet tall or until you run out of materials. Be sure to cover any wet layers of kitchen scraps with soil to discourage odors and flies. To avoid visits by dogs, cats or rodents be sure to make the pile in a bin or wire organizer and cover the top.

Water the compost pile as you would the garden, keeping the material moist but not soaked. To aerate the pile, turn it with a spade or pitchfork, lifting bottom materials to the top to expose the inner materials to air. The pile should be turned after the first week and then once every few weeks over the two to three month period it will take to decompose.

As the organic matter decomposes, heat is produced and is most pronounced in the center of the pile. Children marvel at this phenomenon when they reach in to feel the pile. Once the compost has been properly decomposed, it should look crumbly and dark, should not smell foul and will no longer be hot. If your compost smells bad, chances are that it is too wet or poorly aerated.

COVER CROPPING IS A GOOD PROJECT FOR THE KIDS—EVEN IN SMALL GARDENS

Cover cropping, or *green manuring* as it is sometimes called, means growing and turning under special crops which fertilize the soil and improve its texture. It's a centuries-old practice which can benefit your gardens and teach the youngsters more good gardening techniques.

(Before tackling the project ideas below, read more about cover cropping practices and benefits in *Down-to-Earth Vegetable Gardening Know-How* by Dick Raymond. See Resource section at end of book.)

Ideas for a group project

One project for youngsters is to sow five or six small plots with different cover crops. The plots can be as small as 5 feet by 10 feet.

A selection of crops for spring or early summer planting might include oats, barley, buckwheat, millet, soybeans, field peas, or sorghum.

Late summer or fall crop ideas would include annual ryegrass, winter wheat, winter rye, crimson clover, vetch or kale.

Youngsters should place a sign in every different cover crop plot. Keeping records is a good idea—how much seed used, when the plants first emerged, which crop shaded out weeds the best, and when the crop was turned under.

COVER CROPPING IDEAS
Recommended crops for spring planting

	Seeding Rate lbs./1,000 sq. ft.
Oats	2½
Barley	2½
Buckwheat	2
Millet	1½
Soybeans	3½
Field peas	2½
Sorghum	2½

Recommended crops for fall planting

Annual Ryegrass	1½
Winter wheat	2½
Winter rye	2
Crimson clover	1½
Vetch	1½
Kale	½

DOES YOUR GARDEN SITE REQUIRE A FENCE?

This is a question often asked by groups when developing their new sites. You should consider the following:

*Fencing defines and highlights the garden area. Fences can be used to separate youth gardening activities from other uses of the property.

*The best fences keep woodchucks, rabbits, skunks and other animals out of the garden. Fences discourage random traffic, littering and trespassing through the garden.

*Fences often provide support for vine crops, climbing flowers, and vegetative screens such as ivies or bittersweet. Some fences also serve as windbreaks.

*Fences screen out unwanted sights and sounds from nearby roads and may also screen out pollutants in the air.

*Fences are costly if purchased new and installed by a contractor and many programs can get by without fencing. So, unless you have a serious problem, it may be best to do without one and see what problems come up. After the first season, you might find that a fence is an absolute necessity, or perhaps just a good improvement.

*Many fences can be built with free or low-cost materials—wooden pallets, scrap wood, or used snow fencing from building sites or highway departments.

*Chain link fencing is probably the strongest and longest-lasting kind of fence. It's expensive, though, and that makes it a good focal point for fund-raising.

*We don't recommend using electric fences of any kind in youth garden projects. Even though they are about the only fence to keep racoons and woodchucks out, it's not worth risking an accident with a youngster.

*Fences should have minimum gate widths of 4 feet to allow mowers and wheelbarrows to pass through. Gates get the most wear and tear of any part of a fence, so make sure they are built tough. Gate posts should be dug at least 3 feet down to withstand a lot of strain.

For more information on fence-building, consult *Build It Better Yourself,* Rodale Press.

GETTING WATER TO YOUR GARDEN

We've learned that many garden programs get water at no cost, while others work out agreements to reimburse the landowner or building owner.

If an outdoor water faucet (called a "sill cock" in the plumbing trade) is located on your school or sponsor's building, try to get permission to hook up a garden hose to it.

If necessary, a meter can be added to measure how much water is used. Your local water department has information on the use, purchase and installation of meters.

Vinyl hoses are least expensive but will not last or be as flexible as a well-made rubber or laminated filament hose. If your hose crosses a roadway, use rubber hose to withstand the weight of vehicles. Garden hoses are available in ½-, ⅝- and ¾-inch diameters. A ⅝-inch hose is adequate for most situations.

Soaker hoses made of rubber or plastic can be attached to your main hoses. They are more efficient than sprinklers and can be moved periodically or left in place all season.

Plastic pipe systems are easy to install

If a water source is available from neighboring buildings, but access to the property is difficult, a plastic pipe system is a good way to bring water to the site. A good setup allows for several faucets and lets you control water at the site, rather than way back at the source.

Temporary pipe systems are usually laid out in the spring and broken down and stored during the off-season. In areas of the country where temperatures do not go below freezing, a plastic pipe system can serve as a permanent water line; otherwise, any pipe left out must be drained to prevent its freezing and cracking.

To protect the pipe from accidental cutting or excessive heating, bury the line in a 10- or 12-inch deep trench. Let people know where the pipes are buried so they don't dig too deep in those areas.

Storing water at the garden

If there's no convenient access to water, but a way to fill storage containers from time to time, try using 55-gallon or larger steel or plastic drums or tanks. Be sure, however, that they have not contained toxic substances.

Steel drums can be purchased for $5-15 at scrap metal dealers and industrial supply centers. Be sure drums are thoroughly cleaned out and have no leaks or interior rust.

Drums will collect some rainfall, but they should be filled regularly from a water source.

Community gardens in Boston and Philadelphia have permission to draw from fire hydrants to fill their tanks. At some other gardens, local water departments fill drums from a water tank truck or from hoses running from a nearby building source.

Plastic pipe systems can be attached to any water faucet using a brass adaptor.

Helpful water facts

Under normal conditions, plants require about 1 inch of water or rain per week. The root zones, several inches down, should be soaked well. To check if your garden has received enough water, dig with a trowel or shovel 3 to 6 inches deep to see how well water is moving through the soil.

A rule of thumb in most areas is to check the garden and water as needed once every seven to ten days. You will soon get to know how well your soil absorbs and retains water.

Water is a valuable and limited resource in most places. Give youngsters lessons on proper watering techniques and water conservation methods, such as mulching, so they will use water wisely.

Even areas with abundant rain, such as the Southeastern states, can have severe summer droughts. It's best to plan on supplemental irrigation. Drip irrigation is the most efficient watering system. If you use 100 gallons of water in furrow-style irrigation, only 50 gallons of it gets to the root zone. Sprinklers might deliver 75 of the 100 gallons to the root zone, but drip gets 90 to 95 gallons close to the plants where it is needed.

Eighty to 90 percent of all root growth of most vegetable plants occurs in the uppermost 8 inches of soil.

When possible, irrigate in the late afternoon, early morning, at night, or on cloudy days, to cut potential water losses by evaporation. Best is early in the morning so plants can dry off quickly.

Heat wilt is common, particularly with large-leafed plants such as squash and melons. They will usually perk up after a cool night. If the wilt is still evident by morning, water.

Plants transpire most actively in full sunshine. Therefore, don't cut flowers in full sun as there may not be enough water in the stems to keep flowers from flagging.

EXTEND YOUR SEASON WITH COLDFRAMES

Regardless of the length of your growing season, building and using coldframes can add a nice dimension to your gardening program. A coldframe is essentially a mini-greenhouse and, as such, enables plants to thrive when the outside temperature is too cold for good growth.

Such a structure consists of a frame covered with glass, plastic or fiberglass, which lets in light and traps heat. The construction can be quite simple, with hay bales for walls and an old storm window for the top, or it can be built as a more permanent wooden frame structure.

BOB PEAK

Watering at Evansville, Indiana school

A water-saving tip

"When you water a drought garden by bucket brigade, as I do, you make sure every drop goes where it'll do the most good. Here's how I do it: cut bottoms from plastic milk jugs. Remove caps and countersink, neck down, beside plants. Fill with water as needed.

"Large juice or coffee cans or other suitable containers also can be used. Just punch a few holes in the bottom. Of course, the smaller the container the more often it will need to be filled. Incidentally, it's a good idea to put your jugs in place while plants are small to minimize root disturbance. For large plants like tomatoes, use more than one jug if you have plenty."

M.J. Mears
Augusta, West Virginia
reprinted from Troy-Bilt Owner News
Garden Way Mfg. Co.
Troy, N.Y.

Construction

Building a coldframe can be a good carpentry project for young gardeners. For best retention of heat, the frame should be at least 3 feet by 6 feet with the back wall higher than the front. The top should ideally slant toward the south approximately 1 inch for every foot of width in order to provide the most light when the sun is low.

The construction should be tight enough to keep out wind and cold. Weatherstripping around the top is often used as are thermal blankets for resting over the top on cold nights. The walls of the frame can be insulated with rigid foam insulation or by piling hay or soil up around the outside.

If you choose to use a wood preservative, use a copper napthenate-type material since it is considered safe to use in contact with plants and soils.

Using your coldframe

Coldframes can be used for a number of purposes.

*If you're starting seedlings indoors, they can be 'hardened off' in the coldframe before being transplanted to the outdoor garden. By setting them in a coldframe one to two weeks before transplanting and opening the top more each day, the plants will gradually become accustomed to outdoor growing conditions.

*They can also be valuable for extending the gardening season on either end and might be particularly useful for programs that only operate during the spring and fall. Many cool-weather crops such as lettuce, spinach and radishes can be sown directly or transplanted into the soil in the coldframe for fall, winter and spring harvests.

*You might want to use your basic coldframe as a 'hot bed' which will meet growing conditions in cooler weather better than a coldframe. The frame, in this case, might be set over a pit (approximately 12 inches) that has been filled with decomposing organic matter (manure and hay, for example) and covered with soil. As the organic matter decomposes, heat will be produced and trapped to warm the plants.

Regardless of which you're using, you and the children will have to carefully monitor the needs of your plants. This becomes an excellent opportunity to involve children as observers. One of the main considerations is to be sure that the frames are well vented since temperatures on sunny days in a closed frame can get dangerously high. Tops, except on cold, cloudy days, should generally be left ajar. Frequency of watering will be dependent on weather, sunlight and degree of venting.

This inexpensive coldframe was built by a sixth grade class for starting garden seedlings.

DESIGNING
THE GARDENS

"I would rather grow a spring garden for a learning experience than teach from the finest textbook available and with the most up-to-date demonstration equipment."

David R. Evans, Teacher
Long Junior High School
Cheraw, South Carolina

SITE DESIGNS THAT WORK

A youth garden site may feature much more than individual garden plots. The following site designs offer ideas on the layout of gardens, landscaping and other site features.

This first site plan from Michigan accommodates 36 fairly large student gardens (each 10 feet by 12 feet) and three small demonstration gardens. The circular demonstration gardens are placed in the center of the garden site and planted with herbs, flowers and gourds. Paths measure 5 feet so tools can be easily moved in and out of student gardens. Total area 45 feet by 160 feet.

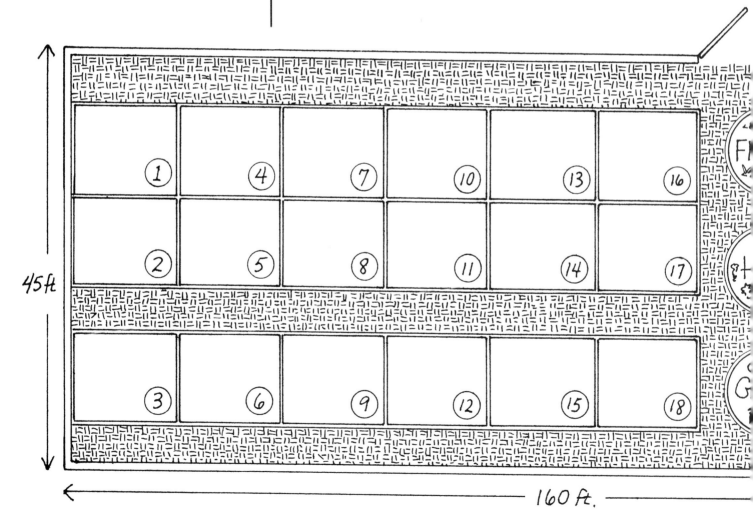

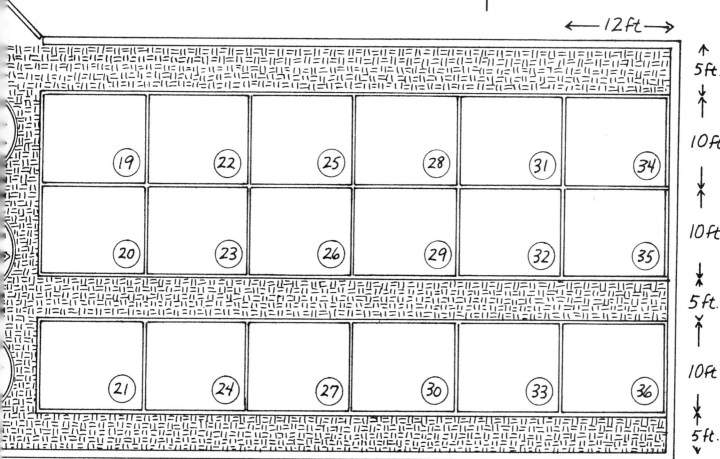

Project Roots

The Neil Armstrong School garden in San Ramon, California contains planting areas of several shapes. Circular beds are good for group projects.

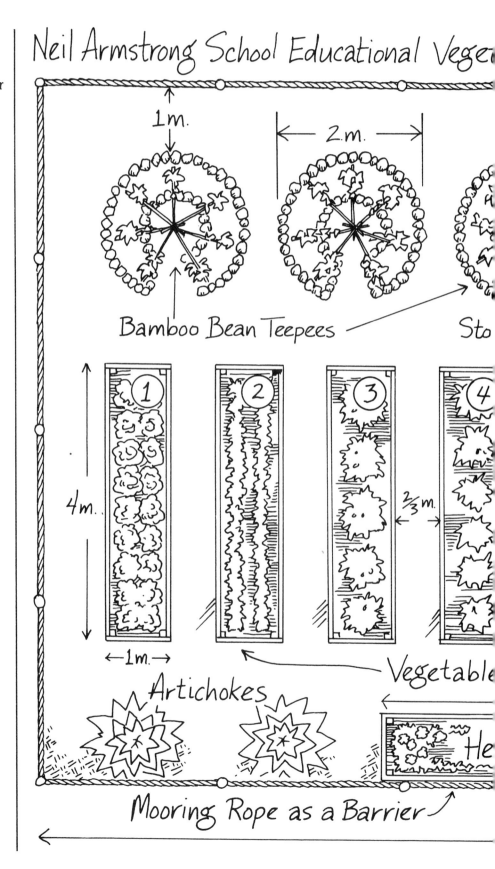

Neil Armstrong School Educational Vege

1 m.

2 m.

Bamboo Bean Teepees

Sto

1

2

3

4

4 m.

⅔ m.

←1m.→

Vegetable

Artichokes

He

Mooring Rope as a Barrier

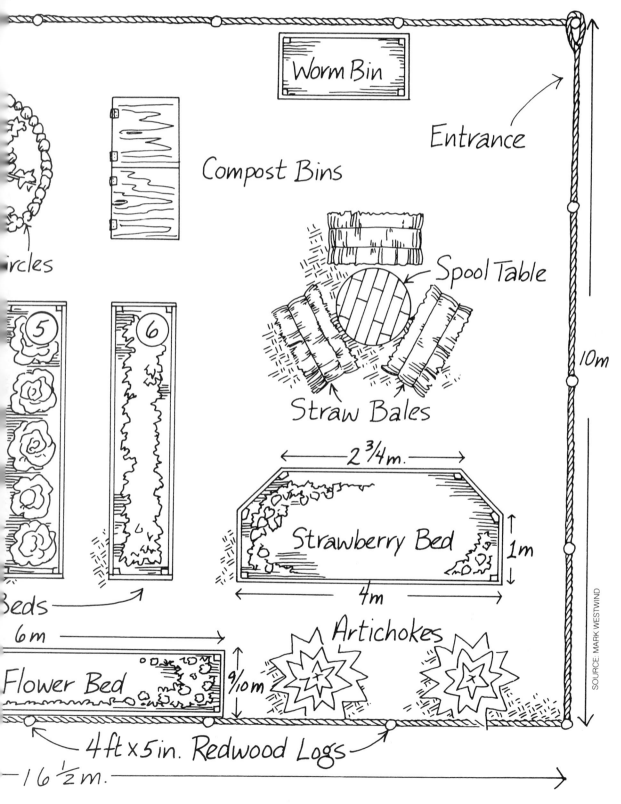

le Garden

Worm Bin

Entrance

Compost Bins

ircles

Spool Table

5

6

Straw Bales

2 ¾ m.

Strawberry Bed

1m

4 m

Beds

10m

6 m

Artichokes

Flower Bed

9/10 m

4 ft × 5 in. Redwood Logs

16 ½ m.

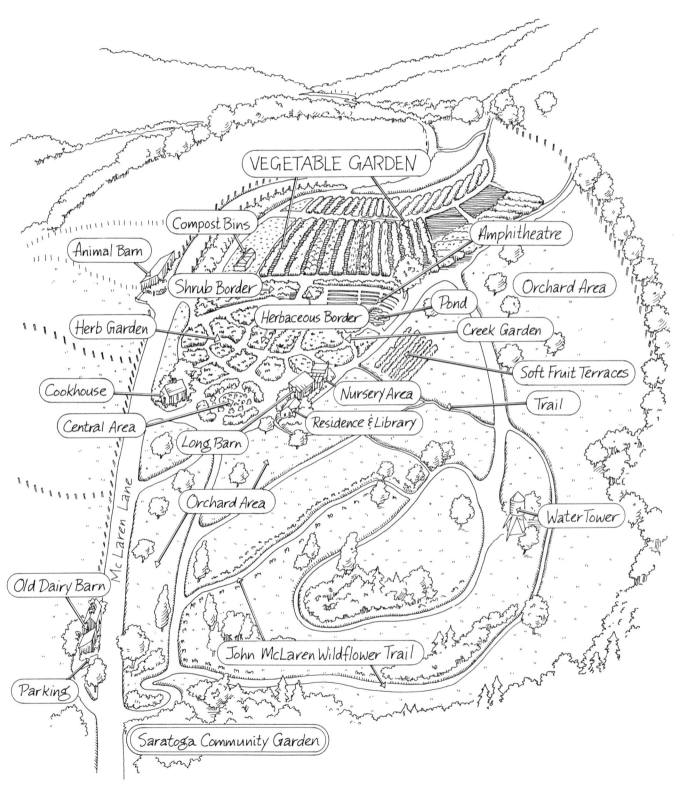

VEGETABLE GARDEN

Compost Bins

Animal Barn

Amphitheatre

Shrub Border

Orchard Area

Herbaceous Border

Pond

Herb Garden

Creek Garden

Soft Fruit Terraces

Cookhouse

Nursery Area

Trail

Central Area

Residence & Library

Long Barn

Orchard Area

Water Tower

Mc Laren Lane

Old Dairy Barn

John McLaren Wildflower Trail

Parking

Saratoga Community Garden

The youth vegetable garden in Saratoga, California is part of a 10-acre complex.

Extra pathways helpful

Young children get so absorbed in gardening that when going for tools or water they'll sometimes walk through a neighbor's garden without thinking. Walkways on all sides of each garden reduce this tendency.

Perimeter pathways reduce soil compaction from foot traffic and also allow plenty of room to move and maneuver tools safely.

Walkways require space, and a path system is usually determined by the size of the site. Four-foot-wide paths are a good minimum because they are wide enough for wheelbarrows. If you have a large site, you might want to consider a 10-foot-wide alleyway through the site, roomy enough for a car or truck to get in and pick up vegetables or deliver supplies.

Of course, added pathways mean extra work. More stakes, string and time are required to set up the site. Also, the more paths you have, the more maintenance is required. It's hard enough to convince some young gardeners to keep their gardens weed-free, but to keep extensive paths maintained as well may be too much.

Paths might be kept weed-free simply from steady foot traffic over them. You also might require that gardeners hoe the pathways near their own gardens. If everyone tends his or her own area well, you won't have a problem of overgrown paths.

Paths can be covered with old carpeting, shredded bark, mulch, or planted with clover or mixed grass seed and then mowed regularly. With more permanent garden sites, materials such as bricks, pebbles, wood chips, crushed stone, or broken concrete can be used for paths, provided they don't hamper tilling.

When covering pathways, first put down some layers of newspapers (no colored ink) or sheets of plastic, then add your mulch, chips, etc. This helps to keep weeds from popping through.

HERE ARE SOME DESIGN IDEAS FOR OPEN SPACE

Communal gardens

If your individual plots are small, plan a common area for crops that require lots of room. Share garden chores as well as the harvest. Corn, squash, pumpkins, or potatoes are good choices for the communal garden. Perennials such as strawberries, raspberries, asparagus, herbs and flowers can be grown, but they require a lot more care.

Demonstration gardens

A good teaching garden, showing different gardening techniques and varieties, is a model and inspiration for inexperienced gardeners. If this garden can be planted a bit earlier than others, you'll be a step ahead in "showing how."

Other Good Design Ideas

- birdhouse
- scarecrow
- earthworm bin
- nature trail
- container plantings
- signs
- tool shed
- play area
- outside sink
- weather station
- food dryer
- landscape planting
- arbor

Work area

A table or bench under a tree can serve as a potting area for transplanting seedlings, cleaning and sorting vegetables, or for arts and crafts projects.

Outdoor classroom/sitting areas

A group of hay bales or short, wide logs are good places to sit for outdoor lessons. In a shady spot, the area makes a good gathering place for the gang on hot days. Don't forget a picnic table—it encourages people to enjoy the harvest fresh out of the garden.

Compost area

Set a spot aside for making compost and storing leaves, wood chips, and other organic matter.

Coldframes

Coldframes are used to start seedlings and as a place for indoor plants to harden off before planting. Most seasonal cold frames are inexpensive and can be built from recycled lumber and old storm windows.

Solar greenhouses

An attached or free-standing solar greenhouse is a great addition for an established, well-supported youth program. Greenhouses need a project leader familiar with greenhouse growing techniques to help build skills and interests of young gardeners. Bordering the Alviso Community Gardens in the San Jose, California area, several small pre-fab type greenhouses were built on elementary school land. The greenhouses are now supervised by school teachers, but both young students and community gardeners use them. Note: we've seen many greenhouses fall into disuse because of poor long-range planning, so think twice before embarking on a greenhouse project.

THESE INDIVIDUAL GARDEN LAYOUTS ARE GOOD!

A garden for spring—5 feet by 5 feet

A spring garden is ideal for a school gardening program that will not continue into summer. Plant these frost-tolerant crops as soon as the soil is dry enough to work. The first pickings should be ready within 2-3 weeks after sowing.

Spring Garden

Broccoli, 4-5 plants

Early Peas, 20-25 seeds

Onions, 15-20 Sets

5 ft.

Kohlrabi, ½ pkt.

Mustard, ½ pkt

Radishes, ½ pkt

Beets, ½ pkt

Cress, ½ pkt

Leaf Lettuce, ½ pkt

5 ft.

Project Roots

56

A garden for variety—8 feet by 7 feet

This plan is designed to give youngsters an opportunity to try growing many different kinds of vegetables in a limited amount of garden space. All of the vegetables and the marigolds are easy to grow, making this an excellent garden plan for young gardeners.

Garden for Variety

1 Tomato · 1 Cherry Tomato · 1 Eggplant · 1 Sweet Pepper

Loose Leaf Lettuce, ½ pkt. · Buttercrunch Lettuce, ½ pkt.

Green Beans, 30-40 seeds

Chinese Pea Pods, 40-50 seeds

Onions, 25-30 sets

Beans, 20-30 seeds · Radishes, 1 pkt. · Swiss Chard, ½ pkt.

Swiss Chard, ½ pkt. · Zucchini, 1 plant

Carrots, ½ pkt

Marigolds, 10-12 plants.

8 ft. · 7 ft.

A long and bountiful harvest—10 feet by 10 feet

Very little space is wasted in this garden because of the close spacing of rows and use of spring crops. Note that two types of lettuce grow next to plants that will require more space as the season progresses. The lettuce will be past its peak by the time the tomatoes need the extra space. Early harvesting of the beets and spinach will likewise give the beans and carrots more growing room. Beans and swiss chard follow the radishes. Strong points of this plan include the marigold border marking the front boundary and the potential for a long, bountiful harvest.

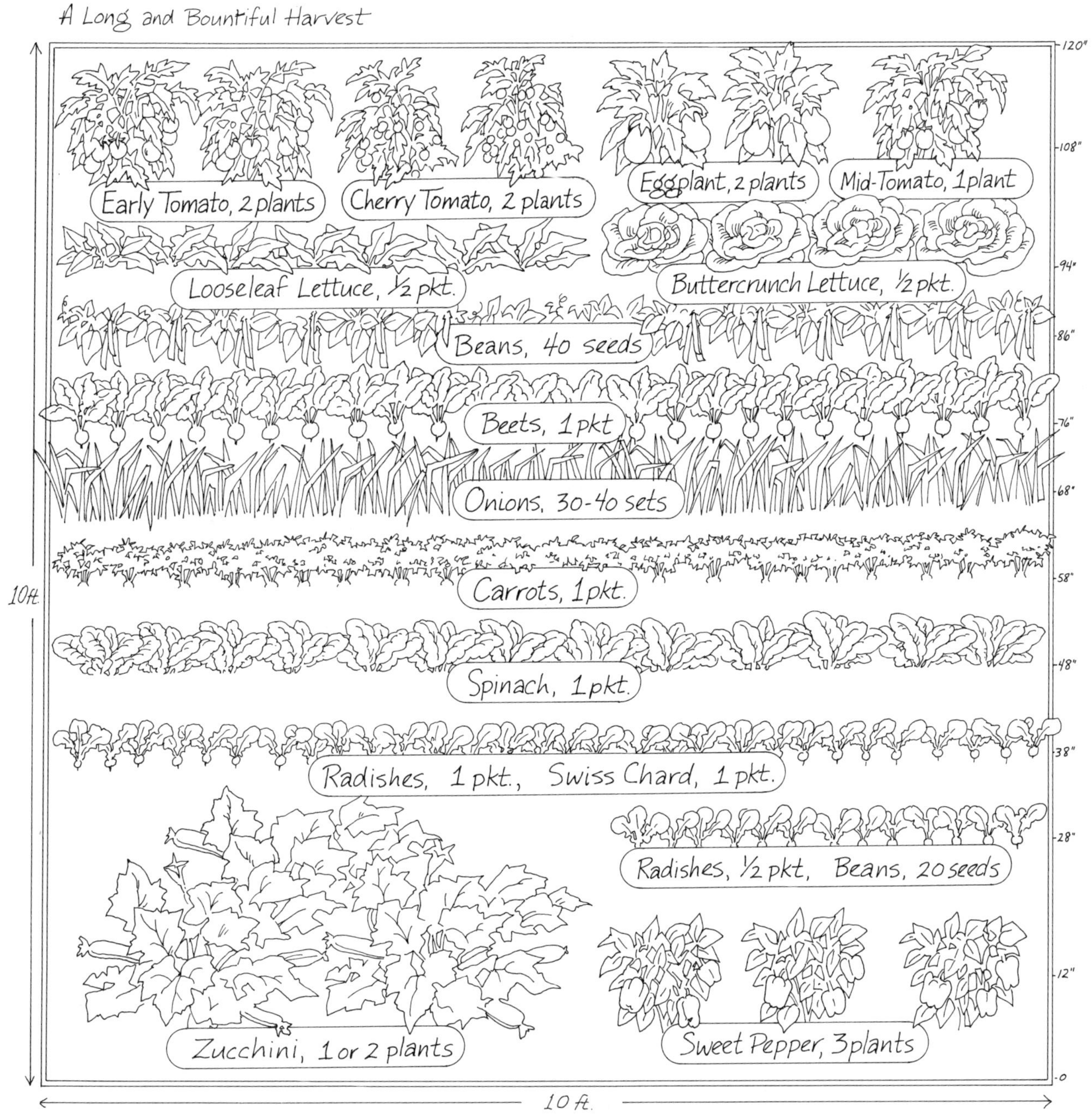

A Long and Bountiful Harvest

Early Tomato, 2 plants

Cherry Tomato, 2 plants

Eggplant, 2 plants

Mid-Tomato, 1 plant

Looseleaf Lettuce, ½ pkt.

Buttercrunch Lettuce, ½ pkt.

Beans, 40 seeds

Beets, 1 pkt

Onions, 30-40 sets

Carrots, 1 pkt.

Spinach, 1 pkt.

Radishes, 1 pkt., Swiss Chard, 1 pkt.

Radishes, ½ pkt, Beans, 20 seeds

Zucchini, 1 or 2 plants

Sweet Pepper, 3 plants

10 ft.

10 ft.

120"

108"

94"

86"

76"

68"

58"

48"

38"

28"

12"

0

HERE'S A GOOD WAY TO MARK OFF PLOTS

Once you've decided on the size of your individual gardens, you should mark off plots before getting the kids involved. Make a sketch of the site boundaries and, if you have a planning committee, ask members to visit the site to look over the different areas where the plots can be laid out.

When starting your first youth program, keep all plots the same size. It's easiest in setting them up if they are all square or rectangle. With same-size gardens, the leader's job is a lot easier as one basic garden plan fits all.

If you use odd-shaped plots, try to have equal square footage for each gardener and easy access around each plot. Each gardener should be able to reach his or her plot without crossing someone else's.

Each plot should be identified by a name, number, flag or other marker. Some leaders place a colored stake in the middle of each plot to avoid confusion because, in the beginning, all plots look the same. Make a note of plot assignments for your own records. A big map for all to see helps.

Step by step

For marking garden plots that are square or rectangular you can use this easy method.

Stake the four corners of your site, carefully checking your dimensions by referring to the plot plan. Then string your garden line to each of these four stakes . Carefully following your paper plan, pound stakes along this boundary line at the points where pathways or ends of gardens are showing . When you are finished you will have stakes at intervals all the way around the garden up against the garden line. Check the dimensions with those on your plan. Then string garden lines between opposite stakes. Do this for the width of the garden and then for the length of the garden, forming a grid of strings over the entire garden area. Finally, pound corner stakes at each point where lines intersect. Once the stakes are in place you can remove the garden lines.

"A PLAN FOR 72 KIDS IN THE GARDEN"

At the National Gardening Association we tested the following garden plan and a group planting technique with 72 first, second, and third graders. We wanted to eliminate the confusion that is common at planting time and enable large groups of children to work successfully with a few adults.

We found that using the following plan, two adults can work well with 25 students at once. Of course, more adults would mean more individualized instruction and a better chance of success for all.

Seventy-two individual gardens were staked out in an area measuring 75 feet by 22 feet. There was also a 25-foot by 30-foot shared garden near the individual gardens.

The individual gardens measured 2 feet by 5 feet and were formed by segmenting five 75-foot-long rows of raised beds. Each row was divided into twelve gardens, with a 5-foot path after every third garden.

Steps in laying out the garden plots

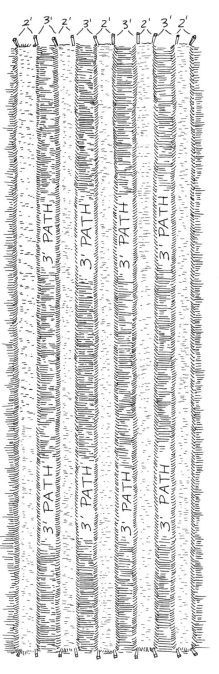

1. To follow this garden plan, first measure and stake out an area 22 feet by 75 feet. String garden line around the garden perimeter. Along the 22-foot dimensions, drive stakes at the following intervals: 2, 5, 7, 10, 12, 15, 17, and 20 feet. String lines between opposite stakes.

2. Using a roto-tiller with a hiller-furrower attachment, till pathways between the strings to form raised beds. It may take several passes with the tiller to raise the beds evenly. You should end up with a 3-foot walkway between each two 75-foot-long beds.

3. When you finish tilling, remove the strings. Along the 75-foot dimensions of the garden, drive stakes at 5-foot intervals. String lines between opposite stakes to create individual gardens. Later when the gardens are planted and seeds have germinated, you can remove the strings that separate the gardens. Until then, it is difficult for the children to distinguish their gardens from the paths. After every third garden, level a 5-foot pathway. You can use the tiller for this, although some hand work is necessary to add finishing touches.

4. At planting time, stretch a string across all of the beds to mark a planting row. All the children plant the same row at the same time. The string is then moved down a few inches to mark the next row. Continue this process until every row is planted.

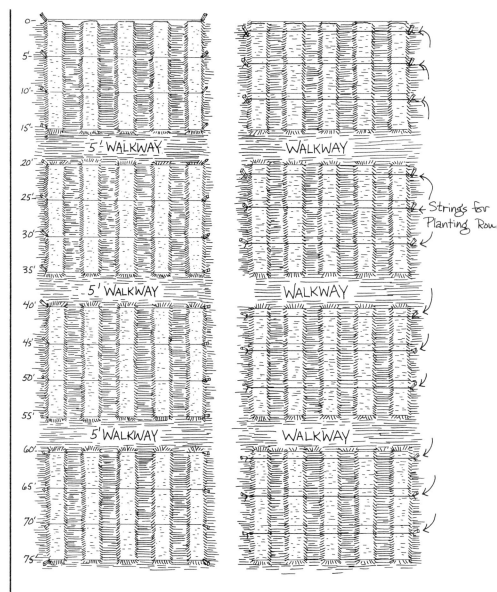

With 2-foot by 5-foot garden plots, the first-time gardeners learned the value of intensive gardening quickly. Each student followed the same garden plan and planted the same crops at the same time. The plan included five rows of vegetables and one of flowers. One of the rows of vegetables was left to student choice. Students planted a row of each of the following: onions, spinach, radishes, and beans. In the "choice rows" students picked from carrots, lettuce, or beets. Some students harvested their onions, radishes, and lettuce and followed with a succession crop. In the row of flowers, students chose two from straw flowers, marigolds, or nasturtiums.

In the 25-foot by 30-foot shared garden students planted peas, tomatoes, cabbage, cauliflower, broccoli, herbs, corn, squash, and pumpkins.

Planting time can be the most exciting part of gardening with children. Just take a little time in advance to explain exactly what they're going to do, and demonstrate each step...then nothing will interfere with their anticipation as they press the seeds of their future gardens into the soil.

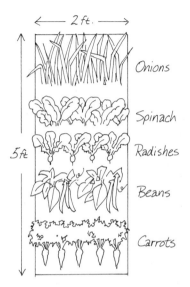

5. Here's a planting scheme for gardens 2 by 5 feet in size.

RAISED BEDS

We used raised bed gardens because they are productive and seeds and plants are not likely to be trampled on by youngsters tending them.

The idea of raised beds is to provide rich, deep, soil that is built up into mounds that are slightly higher than the pathways. Beds are usually 2 or 3 feet wide, and as long as needed. The beds are gardened from both sides, so plants and seedbeds are never walked on.

Important points in raised bed gardening are to add fertilizer and plenty of organic matter during soil preparation, working the soil to a depth of 2 feet or so when adding amendments. This improves drainage, water retention and air flow, and results in healthy, deep root growth by plants.

A raised bed design for asphalt lots

Helen Steer is a carpenter and volunteer with a New York City youth garden project sponsored by the world-wide organization "Save The Children."

She designed the 18 raised, wooden planting beds for vegetables and flowers on what was previously a rubble-strewn vacant lot on East 6th Street between Avenues B and C.

Soil was hauled in to begin the gardens but the 100 or so youngsters involved now do their fertilizing with compost made at the gardens.

They specialize in picking up spoiled or bruised produce from supermarkets and fruit stands. They also bring in organic wastes from home and even save orange peels from school lunches. In the fall, leaves are swept up and hauled to the garden site.

The wooden raised beds are built with an overhang so youngsters and older people can sit comfortably on benches and work around plants.

Raised bed growing on empty New York City lot.

Garden signs can be used to highlight program sponsors.

SIGNS CAPTURE THE SPIRIT OF YOUR GARDEN

Many youth garden groups erect signs to:
*Publicize their sponsors
*Identify the project
*Communicate their feelings about the garden
*Announce hours, tours, or general information
*Provide warnings, rules, guidelines
*Label composting areas and provide instructions
*Explain demonstration plots, perennial plantings
  or vegetable varieties

Signs can be simple—they just need to be clear. Handmade signs can blend in nicely with the natural setting. Recycled or scrap lumber, sanded down, makes a good backing for a painted sign. Your signs can be a good group or class project. You can have kids design a logo or drawings for the sign or invite a talented parent to lend a hand.

Letters can be stencilled on with paint, carved in wood with a chisel or router, drawn free hand, or purchased with paste backings from a hardware store. Use your imagination and folks will take notice of your efforts.

Warning: Some program leaders feel that signs will attract uninvited guests and aren't a good idea in some locations, so discuss the issue of signs with your planning group first.

THE FUN OF GARDENING

"I have been teaching environmental education over the past 5 years and I am beginning to see that a youth garden is one of the most perfect ways of integrating knowledge of the natural world into the curriculum and affecting students' lifestyles and their way of seeing the world. The topics and issues that can be woven into a garden are endless..."

Diana Poslosky, Garden Instructor
John Reed School
Rohnert Park, California

GARDENING ACTIVITIES FOR FUN AND KNOWLEDGE

The activities in this section are a starting point for youngsters to have fun, to learn more about the mystery and fascination of gardens, and to build on their skills of language, science, nutrition and a range of other subjects.

We emphasize "starting point" because almost all of these activities can be expanded or adapted in some way to meet specific teaching needs and curriculum requirements or to fit different age groups. There are endless ways of integrating the garden experience into a daily classroom curriculum. Refer to the 'map' on page 26 and 27 for a visual representation of these possibilities.

The chapter is separated into two parts:

1) This section briefly describes 28 garden tests and experiments which can be used to actively engage children in the scientific process as they learn some important gardening principles.

2) This expanded section describes 70 exciting activities that incorporate a diversity of skills and subject areas. The projects are geared primarily for gardeners 6 to 14 years of age. We have adapted some from outside sources and developed others from experience. All sources, except those no longer readily available, are listed in the resource section of this book.

Two points to remember: look for the time of year recommendation accompanying each activity to help you plan your sessions. Where possible, stress the gardening concepts underlying the activities. It's important that youngsters keep in sight the connection between the activity and the garden.

Time of year recommendations:
1 = anytime
2 = before outdoor planting
3 = during the growing season
4 = after the growing season

We have ended with a list of some other activity ideas which we hope will generate excitement and spark many new ideas on your part.

28 GARDEN EXPERIMENTS AND TESTS

Here's a list of gardening projects to perk up the interest of young gardeners and teach them some important gardening principles.

1. Spacing of onion sets

Plant three short rows of onion sets. Place sets in one row 2 inches apart, in the next 4 inches apart, and in the third 6 inches apart. Fertilize and water all rows equally. Record the number of onions in each row, the weight of onions after harvesting, and the biggest individual onion. Which row did the largest come from?

2. Bean seeds

Count out 60 bean seeds of the same variety. Plant 20 of them 2 inches apart in a row. Plant 20 seeds each 4 inches apart in another row; plant the last 20 seeds 8 inches apart in a row. Make observations on how the plants grow, if they shade out the ground, and the amount of harvest from each row.

3. Wide row lettuce

Plant a single row of lettuce about 5 feet long. Next to it, plant a wide row of lettuce 5 feet long by about 15 inches wide. (Sprinkle the seeds to plant.) How much seed is used for each? Which is easier to thin out? To weed? Which produces the most lettuce per foot of row?

4. Transplanting cabbage

Take eight cabbage transplants ready to be set out in the garden. On four of them, pinch off all leaves but one. Do not pinch out the center sprout. On the other four, don't take any leaves off. Treat all plants the same after that. Note which plants respond best to the shock of transplanting. Which plants grow fastest? Produce the first heads?

5. Block planting

Plant a block of peas or beans. String off a 5-foot by 5-foot section of garden. Don't use any walkways inside. Sprinkle the seeds about 3 or 4 inches apart all over the block and rake them into the soil. Don't do any weeding. Watch how the plants grow up close to each other and prevent weeds from growing.

6. Swiss chard harvest

Harvest part of your Swiss chard rows by cutting off the entire plant about 1 or 2 inches above the soil. Watch it grow back and compare the tenderness of leaves with the section of row you harvest by picking the outside leaves of plant.

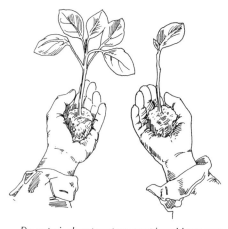

Do not pinch out center sprout in cabbage test.

23. Compacted soil

Plant two 5-foot-long rows of lettuce or radishes, about 3 or 4 feet apart. After planting both rows normally, ask someone to walk over one of them, stepping down hard. Don't walk over the other seedbed. Which plants come up first? Why?

24. Tomato transplanting techniques

When you're transplanting tomatoes, try two different methods. Put 4 or 5 plants of a variety in the ground *horizontally,* stripping the bottom leaves and covering the stem with about 3 inches of soil. Put an equal number of plants of the same variety in the ground *vertically,* sinking the root ball down 4 or 5 inches. Which plants blossom first? Which yield the first harvest? Note other differences between the groups. (At the end of the season you can dig up the horizontally-planted tomatoes and examine the root growth along the buried stem.)

25. Black plastic and melons

Plant a few melons through a tight mulch of black plastic. Plant some normally in unmulched soil. Does the black plastic make a difference in yields? What about in weeding and watering?

26. Carrots and thinning

Plant two rows of carrots. Thin out one row as you would normally. Don't thin the other row. When you start harvesting from the first row, pull up some plants in the other row. Does thinning affect the size and shape of the carrots?

Two ways to set tomatoes into the garden.

27. Companion planting

Try some companion planting schemes to make pests bug off. Around some tomato plants, for example, plant dill and marigolds. Compare them later with tomatoes without companion crops near them. Any difference in pest problems? Try other variations around cabbage plants, eggplants and beans. One youth leader suggests growing a few tobacco plants as a "bug-trap" lesson; also, grow a few borage plants near cucumber rows to attract bees.

28. Plant protectors

Plant two separate 'hills' of squash with three seeds in each hill. Cover the seeds in one hill with mini-greenhouses or hot caps made by cutting the bottoms from plastic milk cartons. Which seeds germinate more quickly? Provide ventilation by removing the lids on the cartons and watch for the differences in growth between the covered and uncovered seedlings.

GARDEN ACTIVITIES

The Garden Journal (1)

Each gardener should keep a journal of his or her garden activities, observations, and feelings. Drawings, poetry, stories and other projects can all be done in the journal. Journals are a place for personal reflection or focusing one's own interests. This project becomes a reference for the children, and is something they will keep long after the garden goes by.

Set aside a time each week for journal writing. Between these times, when some kids finish projects or garden activities before others, they can work in their journals and keep busy in a constructive way.

Making a garden journal can be a project in itself, or you can purchase 8½-by 11-inch binders and fill them with paper. Binders with a pocket are good for keeping pencils or crayons. Children can decorate the covers of their journals with a collage or original drawings.

Find the Hidden Words (1)

Construct an anagram, or word scramble, of garden words and give one to each youngster with a list of the words to find and circle. When they have found all the words, discuss and define them.

When the children get the hang of this game, see if they can construct an anagram themselves, either individually or as a group.

The following words are in the word scramble. They can be found either horizontally or vertically, spelled forward or backward.

Rake
Shovel
Hoe
Tomato
Lettuce
Seeds
Leaves
Plant
Corn
Pea
Worm
Row
Thin

U	K	R	S	P	E	A
C	G	A	T	V	P	L
D	L	K	R	P	L	N
S	E	E	D	S	A	M
H	T	H	I	N	N	R
O	T	O	M	A	T	O
V	U	E	A	F	G	W
E	C	O	R	N	D	O
L	E	A	V	E	S	R

1 = anytime 2 = before outdoor planting 3 = during the growing season 4 = after the growing season

Garden Riddles (1)

This activity is designed for grade levels one through four.

What to do:

Divide the group into two-person teams. Assign each team the job of creating a riddle dealing with the garden or the environment. Each group should write its riddle on paper and read it. The rest of the group must solve the riddle.

Some examples:

Though I am small,
I'm really strong.
Give me dirt and water
And I'll perform.
What am I?   (a seed)

I'm round and pink
with fuzz on my cheeks.
What am I?   (a peach)

I'm not too old
but have lots of wrinkles
and some say
I'm plum cute!!
What am I?   (a prune)

I have eyes
but cannot see.
Dig me up for vitamin C.
What am I?   (a potato)

If you cut me,
I'll make you cry.
What am I?   (an onion)

I always grow beneath the ground.
Pull me from above,
I'm easily found.
What am I?   (a root)

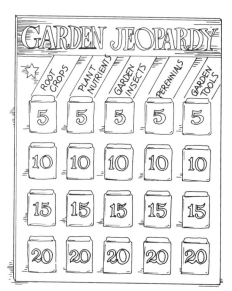

"Root crops for 10 points!"

Garden Jeopardy (1)

This game, based on the TV quiz show, helps to reinforce gardening concepts.

Things you need:
*Vegetable jeopardy board
*60 jeopardy question/answer cards

What to do:
1. Construct the game using 22-inch by 28-inch poster board.
2. Attach 20 library book pockets (four rows, five in each row.) Label chart according to diagram.
3. Cut question/answer cards and place them in appropriate pockets.
4. Divide the group into four or five teams. Garden leader can act as moderator.
5. A member of the first team (every team member takes a turn) looks at the board and chooses a category and the number of points he or she wants to try for. For example: "root crops for 10 points." The monitor selects a card from the category and point level chosen and reads the "answer" to the player. If the player gives the correct "question," the team scores the points indicated on the card and the card is put aside. An incorrect answer scores no points.
6. Students can make up questions of their own to add to the game. Correct answers must be given using the jeopardy format, "What is/are _____?"

Source: "Peanut Butter and Pickles"
Humboldt County
Office of Education, 901 Myrtle Ave.,
Eureka, California 95501

1 = anytime 2 = before outdoor planting 3 = during the growing season 4 = after the growing season

World Hunger Activity (1)

This activity will help children become familiar with the inequality of distribution of food in the world.

Things you need:
   *Enough apples to provide each person with one apiece.
   *A paring knife.

What to do:
   1. In advance, divide the apples so that roughly one quarter of the children will receive nothing or only small bits of apple, roughly one quarter will receive a very small portion (one slice), roughly one quarter will receive a moderate portion (three slices each), roughly one quarter will receive a very large portion (10 slices each) and a small percent (one person) will receive 25 slices.
   2. Explain that you will be serving a snack that reflects how much people around the world get to eat. Mention also that the world actually *does* produce enough to feed every person the equivalent in calories to what the average U.S. citizen eats every day. Distribute the apple pieces randomly so that those receiving large portions are close to those receiving small portions or nothing.
   3. Explain how this distribution corresponds to that in the real world. Have the group discuss whether it would like to see the food distributed differently. If so, let them try to design a fair method.
   4. Allow the children to eat. Discuss the process and how it relates to the real world, how the children with the biggest portions feel, how those with the smallest portions feel, how the world might be able to equalize the availability of food.
   5. Discuss the existence of hunger in your area, the children's experiences with hungry people, the possible causes of hunger, and possible solutions. Allow the children to make journal entries on how it felt to be a part of the simulation and about their resulting thoughts.

adapted from:
"Food First
Curriculum"
by Laurie Rubin
Institute for Food and Development Policy

ANGOON, AK SCHOOLS

1 = anytime 2 = before outdoor planting 3 = during the growing season 4 = after the growing season

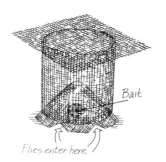

Backyard flytrap can be used where flies are a problem.

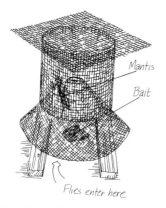

Stinky bait attracts flies for praying mantis to eat.

Build a Home for Your Praying Mantis (2)

The praying mantis gets its name from its forelegs, which make the insect look as if it's praying. The mantises are predators—they eat other insects in the garden, many of which can pester vegetable crops.

The mantises do not have a larval and pupal stage like butterflies; their eggs hatch directly into a form similar to the adult. There are usually three molts, or sheddings of skin as they mature into adults.

What to do:

1. To raise praying mantises, first get some mantis egg cases. Look in garden magazines for sources or send for a catalog from Mellinger's Supply, 2310 W. South Range Road, North Lima, OH 44452.
2. Keep the egg cases where you can check them regularly. The hatching young should be removed from the cluster each day or the older ones will eat them as they emerge.
3. As the little eggs hatch, youngsters can take them home in paper cups and release them in the garden where there are vegetables.
4. You can rear some mantises in cages. It's a challenge because their food has to be other live insects, but it can be done in several ways:
   A. Use a cage for the mantisorium with a screen coarse enough to allow other insects to enter. Place a piece of banana, foul meat, or anything to attract insects through the cover.
   B. Another good rearing cage is a backyard flytrap. Use one wherever flies are a problem.
   C. A simple form of flytrap is made by placing a cylinder of wire loosely over a wire cone. Place some stinky bait under the cone and prop up the edges to let the flies in. They try to leave by crawling up and thus become food for the praying mantis.

Source: Burnell Yarick
Men's Garden Club
Glendale, California

Praying mantis

Egg case

1 = anytime 2 = before outdoor planting 3 = during the growing season 4 = after the growing season

Where Does Food Come From? (2)

Knowing which food comes from which plant is a matter of experience, especially in the case of fruits, nuts and vegetables. This lesson expands awareness of food sources and is a good one for discussion.

Things you need:
*Magazines and seed catalogs for pictures
*Poster board
*Tape or glue
*Felt pens

What to do:
1. Explain that the foods we eat may be the fruit of a tree; the fruit, leaves, stem, root or seed of a bush or small plant; or a product of the ocean or an animal. Pass out magazines and seed catalogs and ask the children to cut out pictures of different foods.
2. As a group, look at these pictures and determine the source of each food. If there is a picture of a loaf of bread, ask what plant parts it's made of and what particular plant it's from. (This may be more difficult than tracing the origins of the vegetable and fruit pictures.)
3. List on a poster different sources of food: grasses, trees, animals, etc. or leaves, fruits, roots, etc., and illustrate each with an example. Then have the children post their magazine pictures underneath the right source. If there are mistakes, discuss the food origins and clarify misunderstandings.
4. Follow-up possibilities: Ask the children to pay attention at home to the foods they eat and where they come from. Have them bring in lunches and answer questions such as: Who is eating ground seeds? (bread, peanut butter, etc.) Who is eating fruits? (jelly, tomato soup, etc.)

LINDA LUTZ

*Adapted from: "Edible City
Resource Manual"
William Kaufman, Inc.
Los Altos, California*

1 = anytime 2 = before outdoor planting 3 = during the growing season 4 = after the growing season

Watch Roots Grow (2)

A root-view box can be built many different ways, but the viewing area should always be covered well except at viewing times.

Things you need:
*Half-gallon milk carton
*Sheets of acetate (such as kind used in making overhead projector transparencies)
*Carrot, onion or bean seeds
*Waterproof glue or pruning paint

What to do:
1. Use the milk carton vertically, and cut a large window on one side. Leave about one-half inch of carton between seams and window.
2. Cut the acetate to fit the window and glue it in place from inside the carton.
3. When the glue is dry, fill the carton with moist soil mix and plant seeds of your choice close to the window.
4. Tip the carton over slightly toward the window side and support it there to keep roots growing straight down toward the window.
5. Tape the cut out carton piece, or a piece of construction paper, to the window to keep light from hitting the soil. Lift the window covering only at viewing times.

Tip:
*Compare top and root growth of vegetables of different varieties, or the growth of vegetables in different soils and mixes.

—Window

Pickle a Cucumber in a Bottle (3)

Things you need:
*A young cucumber growing on the vine
*A small-necked bottle with cork top or other lid
*Newspaper
*Pickling brine (½ salt, ½ water, for preservation only, not for later eating.)

What to do:
1. When a cucumber first forms on a vine slip it into a small-necked bottle. As it grows it will expand inside the bottle.
2. Protect the bottle from the sun with a few sheets of newspaper, otherwise it will get too hot for the cuke.
3. When the cucumber nearly fills the bottle, cut the vine and you will have a mystery to share with your friends. Pick the cucumber before it gets too big or it may break the glass.
4. When you harvest the bottled cuke, pour a basic brine mixture into the bottle and cork the top. It will last a long time!

Newspaper keeps cuke in bottle from getting too hot.

1 = anytime 2 = before outdoor planting 3 = during the growing season 4 = after the growing season

Recycle Some Garbage (2)

This project shows how organic matter will break down into compost over a period of weeks. The bacteria in this "mini-compost" bag need air to work on the organic matter.

Things you need:
*Organic matter (leaves, grass clippings, banana peels, citrus fruit peels, apple cores without seeds, coffee grounds, potato peels, wood ashes, etc.)
*Plastic baggies
*Twist ties
*Garden soil
*Alfalfa meal or unused "Litter Green" kitty litter
*Water

What to do:
1. Label a baggie with your name and date. Add 1 cup of organic matter to the baggie. Tear up the organic matter into small pieces.
2. Add ½ cup of garden soil to the baggie.
3. Add 1 tablespoon alfalfa meal or "Litter Green" kitty litter (100% alfalfa pellets).
4. Add an ounce of water to the mixture. Seal the baggie.
5. Mix all the materials together by shaking the baggie.
6. Squeeze the baggie daily to mix contents.
7. Every other day open the bag for the day.
8. If contents smell, something is wrong. The bag may have too much water or it needs air or mixing.
9. Your compost will be ready to use in approximately four to six weeks.

Tip:
In some of the bags, try adding some things that are not organic matter (styrofoam, plastic cups, etc.). Have the children predict what might happen in the different bags. At the end, note the differences in the bags. Discuss and identify substances in our environment that will not break down. Are there other ways of recycling them?

Save lunch peelings for compost.

1 = anytime 2 = before outdoor planting 3 = during the growing season 4 = after the growing season

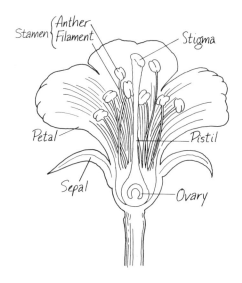

Stamen {Anther, Filament} Stigma

Petal

Pistil

Sepal

Ovary

CLAY RECIPE:

Ingredients:
2½ c flour
½ c salt
1 Tbsp alum
2 c boiling water
3 Tbsp vegetable oil
¼ tsp food coloring

1. **Mix dry ingredients**
2. **Mix food coloring with boiling water.**
3. **Add vegetable oil to water (it won't mix).**
4. **Add liquid to dry ingredients. Mix quickly to moisten all dry ingredients.**
5. **Pour onto a counter and knead until smooth.**
6. **Store in airtight container.**

Recipe Source:
Project ROOTS Lansing, Michigan

Flower Dissection (2) (3)

Learning the basic parts of a flower is as important as learning about the basic structures of human and animal physiology. It is also fun for the children to realize that even though flowers may vary greatly, they still have certain structures in common.

Things you need:
*Flowers
*Razor blade

What to do:

1. Cut a flower in half with a razor blade and show the cross section to the children. Have them identify the primary parts (sepal, stamen, petals, pistil). Give a flower to each person and have them pull off the flower parts, one by one.
2. Starting from the stem, the first parts to identify are the sepals. These are usually green, looking like modified leaves. Directly above the sepals are the petals. The main function of petals is to attract insects with their bright colors. In searching for food, the insects are attracted to the petals and inadvertently pollinate the plants.
3. Further inside the flower, find the stamens. These are the male portions of the flower, and carry pollen on their tips (anthers).
4. At the center of the flower is the pistil. This is the female part of the flower, and it collects pollen at its top (stigma). These are often sticky so they more effectively hold on to the pollen. Have the children examine the cross section of the pistil again, more closely this time, to identify the ovary with developing seeds inside.
5. Follow-up. Have the children bring in flowers from indoors and out and try to identify the various parts. Look at flowers from plants such as corn that are wind pollinated and discuss why the showy petals are not necessary. Look at different squash flowers to distinguish between the male and female flowers. (The female flowers have a swollen section—the developing ovary—at the base.)

Tips:
*Use a hand lens to magnify small flower parts
*This exercise can precede a project for making flowers using homemade clay.
*Clay recipe in the margin

Story Hour (3)

Many children love reading to each other, and story time is a great break from the physical work of gardening on a hot summer's day. Find a shady spot near the garden, form a circle, and pass around the garden book of your choice.

Tips:

*If possible, the children should get books of their choice from the library to read.

*Supplement their choices with some "crowd pleasers." Following are a few suggestions. (Note: if the book is still in print, the publisher's address is included. If not, the library would be your best bet.)

Corn is Maize: The Gift of Indians, by Aliki. (grades K-3). Harper and Row Publications, Inc., Keystone Industrial Park, Scranton, PA 18512. $4.95.

Secret Garden, by Francis H. Burnett. (grade 4 and up). Dell Publishing Co., Inc., 1 Dag Hammarskjold Plaza, 245 E. 47th St., New York, NY 10017. $3.50

The Pumpkin People, by David and Maggie Cavagnaro. (grades K-3). Charles Scribner's Sons, 597 Fifth Ave., New York, NY 10017. $8.95

Eddie's Green Thumb, by Carolyn Haywood. (grades 3-7). William Morrow and Co., Inc.

The Beetle Bush, by Beverly Keller. (grades K-3). Coward, McCann and Geoghegan, Inc.

Willie's Garden, by Myra McGee. (grade 5 and up). Rodale Press, Inc.

My Garden, by Louise Murphy. (grades 1-6). Charles Scribner's Sons.

Mr. Plum's Paradise, by Elisa Trimby. (grades K-3). William Morrow and Co., Inc.

This Year's Garden, by Cynthia Ryant and Mary Szilagyi. (grades K-3). Bradbury Press, 866 3rd Ave., New York, NY 10022. $12.95.

1 = anytime 2 = before outdoor planting 3 = during the growing season 4 = after the growing season

80

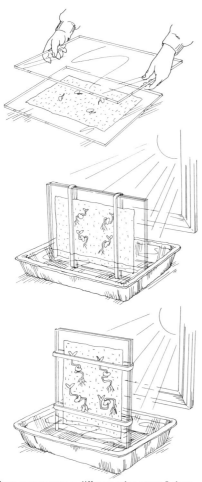

Turn panes onto a different edge every 2 days.

Zig-Zagging Seed (2)

This simple project shows how the force of gravity affects the way in which roots grow.

Things you need:
> *Handful of pre-sprouted seeds (radishes, cucumbers or melons work well)
> *Two panes of glass or plexiglass
> *Blotter paper or paper towel
> *Tray of water
> *Rubber bands

What to do:
1. Lay pre-sprouted seeds on a sheet of blotting paper or paper towel between the two panes of glass or plexiglass. Space them at least an inch apart.
2. Use rubber bands to keep the panes fairly tight together so the seeds don't move when you stand them up.
3. Put the panes upright in a tray of water near a window or grow lights.
4. Rotate the panes onto a different edge every two days. The roots will always grow downwards and the stem will shoot upwards!

The Mysterious Feely Box (2) (3)

The "Feely Box" is a useful tool to build sensory awareness and verbal skills. Games can be played using the box. One example is to place a variety of seeds, leaves, or other garden items in the box, not letting the children see them. Have one child place his or her hand in the box and feel one of the items. By explaining how it feels (not what it looks like), the rest of the group tries to guess the item. The person who guesses correctly then has a turn at feeling and explaining the next object.

Things you need:
> *Corrugated cardboard box
> *Utility knife
> *Plain paper to wrap the box
> *Glue and tape
> *Old seed catalogs
> *A cut-off pant leg or sleeve, heavy thread and needle (optional)

What to do:
1. Tape the empty box closed and wrap it with plain paper.
2. Cut a 3½ inch diameter hole out of the center on one side of the box.
3. Decorate all sides of the box with a collage of vegetable and flower pictures from old seed catalogs.
4. If desired, attach an old pant leg to the hole by sewing through the cardboard with a big needle and heavy thread. This makes the contents more "secretive."

1 = anytime 2 = before outdoor planting 3 = during the growing season 4 = after the growing season

Colorful, Waterproof Row Markers (2) (3)

Things you need:
*Seed packets
*Coat hangers
*Plastic photo album sheets for prints sized 3 by 5 inches

What to do:
1. Take a wire coat hanger and cut wire on both sides, 7 inches from center where both wires twist together.
2. Reshape wire with about 3½ inches between tines.
3. Carefully cut plastic album page into 5 envelopes.
4. Slide a wire fork into each plastic envelope and slide seed packet into plastic envelope.
5. If you have some side-opening plastic envelopes, tape up the long side and use the envelope vertically so rain can't get in.

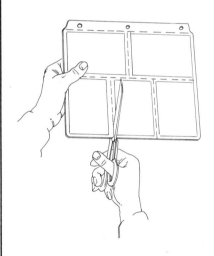

Special T-Shirts for Everyone (2) (3)

Making garden club t-shirts gives children a feeling of really belonging to the garden group.

Things you need:
*Each child should bring in a white t-shirt. (If new, it should be washed first so the design will adhere to the shirt)
*Permanent ink markers
*Fabric paints (available at hobby stores)

What to do:
1. Stuff a sheet of cardboard into the shirt and lay it flat on a table. This will prevent ink and paint from soaking through from one side to the other.
2. Following a garden theme, have the children create a design on paper. This drawing becomes the plan for them to follow in transferring it onto the t-shirts. The outlines can be filled in with fabric paints.
3. There are several ways to transfer the design. Here are a few:
   A. Children can draw onto their own t-shirt.
   B. They can outline around cardboard cut-outs.
   C. If the t-shirts are light enough, the design drawn on paper may be inserted inside, on top of the cardboard, so that it can be seen through the fabric and the children can trace over it.

Tip:
Important: Designs must be ironed before children wear the t-shirts. The heat sets the fabric paint so it doesn't fade or run.

1 = anytime 2 = before outdoor planting 3 = during the growing season 4 = after the growing season

Make a Toad House (3)

A friendly toad will gobble up many harmful bugs that come into your garden. You can try to get toads to move in by making toad houses.

Things you need:
   *Scissors
   *Two plastic cottage cheese containers

What to do:
1. Carefully cut a half-circle doorway out of the top edge of one cottage cheese container. The opening should be big enough for a toad to fit through.
2. Turn this container upside down, near the edge of your garden. This is the toad's house.
3. Next to the toad house dig a hole big enough for the other container to fit in, right-side-up. Fill this container with water and it becomes the toad's swimming pool.
4. Now the house is all ready. Put a sign outside the house, "Toad House for Rent," and hope a toad moves in.

1 = anytime 2 = before outdoor planting 3 = during the growing season 4 = after the growing season

Blackberry Jamming (3)

Arrange to use a school's equipment and facilities, or do your jamming at someone's home or at a local community center.

Things you need:
- *Sterilized canning jars
- *5 cups of washed blackberries
- *A stove
- *Large saucepan and lid
- *3 cups of honey
- *Double boiler
- *Paraffin
- *Hot pads

What to do:
1. Gather the materials, some enthusiastic young gardeners and find an available kitchen. Be sure to mention the need for caution with hot stuff. Decide how sweet you want the jam to be, and add enough honey to the blackberries.
2. In a large saucepan bring the blackberries and honey to a quick boil, and continue cooking for 8-10 minutes, stirring occasionally. Let cool for several hours.
3. One hour before going home, sterilize the jars with boiling water, and add jam to within ½-inch of the top.
4. Melt a block of paraffin in the double boiler, and pour a ⅛-inch layer of paraffin on the top of the jam. If jelly bubbles through the paraffin, add another thin layer of paraffin.
5. Label the jar with the name and date, and place in storage.
6. Discuss why it is important to wash the fruit. Why do we add honey to the jam? Why do we need to sterilize the jars? Why is store-bought jam so expensive? Why does store-bought jam often include preservatives, artificial flavors, and artificial color? How much energy might we save if we make the jam ourselves?

Tips:
- *Take some of the home-made jam to other youth groups or classes.
- *Explain how it was made. Have kids draw a step-by-step diagram to help interested folks understand the process.

Source: "Edible City Resource Manual"
William Kaufman, Inc.
Los Altos, California

1 = anytime 2 = before outdoor planting 3 = during the growing season 4 = after the growing season

84

Japanese beetle trap needs beetle lure (available at many garden stores).

Build a Japanese Beetle Trap (3)

This is an easy, cheap way to make an effective Japanese beetle trap which works just as well as any store-bought trap.

Things you need:
*2-liter plastic soda or tonic bottle
*Section of old mesh onion bag
*Japanese beetle sex attractant lure (about $4 at garden centers)
*Jar lid
*Stapler, scissors or Exacto knife, screwdriver and light hammer
*Piece of wire

What to do:
1. Cut three openings in the tonic bottle, each 4 inches by 4 inches, leaving a 1-inch strip between the openings.
2. Out of an onion bag, make a holder for the beetle lure approximately an inch in diameter, 4 inches long. Staple it shut and hang inside the tonic bottle by a piece of wire.
3. Make a 1-inch hole in a mayonnaise type jar lid with screwdriver and hammer. Insert narrow opening of tonic bottle in jar cover. That's the receptacle for the beetles that are caught.
4. Make two holes in the tonic bottle, near the top of your trap, and bend a piece of wire to make a handle for hanging up the trap.

*Source: Donald Grahn
Westminster, Mass.*

Pumpkin 4 weeks after being autographed

Grow Your Name on a Pumpkin (3)

Grow a pumpkin patch large enough for all gardeners to get a pumpkin to inscribe.

Things you need:
*A ballpoint pen
*A young pumpkin growing on the vine

What to do:
Sign your name and the date on a young pumpkin with a ballpoint pen, breaking the skin slightly. As the pumpkin grows, so will your name.

1 = anytime 2 = before outdoor planting 3 = during the growing season 4 = after the growing season

85

Naming the Biggest, Smallest and Most Interesting (3)

What to do:
1. Discuss various parts of speech with the students (for example, adjectives and adverbs), and talk about how they can help us describe or define things. Discuss the ways we can tell what someone is talking about even when they haven't named the object outright.
2. Tell the class that they will have five minutes in the garden. During this time, they are to find what they think is (1) the smallest object (living or non-living) in the garden, (2) the largest object in the garden, and (3) the most interesting object in the garden. Tell them they must use this time to discover everything they can about these three objects—how they look, feel, smell, what they do, etc.
3. Take the students to the garden for the allotted time, leaving all possible distractions behind.
4. When the students return to the classroom, have them write a paragraph on each of the three objects they observed. At the end of the paragraph, have them name what they were observing. (Don't name the object in the paragraph itself.)
5. Before the papers are handed in, have each child read one of his or her paragraphs aloud, omitting the actual naming of the object. Let the other students guess what is being described.

Grow Plants in a Maze (2)

Light, or its absence, affects the way a plant grows. The maze shows the concept of "phototropism" as the plant grows toward its light source.

Things you need:
*Sprouting potato
*Small pot of moist soil mix to fit the potato
*Shoe box and two pieces of cardboard

What to do:
1. Take a potato that has sprouted a couple of inches and plant it in the pot of moist soil mix.
2. Put the pot in the corner of a shoe box, then cut a hole at the other end of the shoe box.
3. Tape two partitions in the box, one starting at the box top and stopping short of the bottom, the other fastened to the bottom of the box and stopping 2 inches short of the top.
4. Now close the box and set it next to the window. A chemical called "auxin" in the young plant influences it to grow toward the light, through the "maze."

Potato sprouts will seek light through a maze.

1 = anytime 2 = before outdoor planting 3 = during the growing season 4 = after the growing season

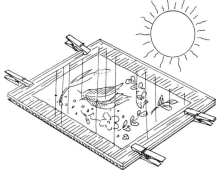

Don't expose blueprint paper to light before making prints.

Natural Blueprints from the Garden (3)

This activity is quick (10 minutes or so to set up and make each print) and lots of fun. Leaves of vegetable plants will yield a finely-detailed print, good enough for plant identification exercises.

Things you need:
*Blueprint paper (cut into 8½-by 11-inch pieces) available from architects or drafting supply houses. Since this is light-sensitive paper, work with it as quickly as possible and do not expose it to direct light until step 5.
*Heavy cardboard (cut into 12-inch by 12-inch pieces)
*Clothespins (clip-on type)
*Light source
*Leaves, flowers, weeds, grains from garden
*Plexiglas (cut into 12-inch by 12-inch pieces), available from hardware store or art supply store

What to do:
1. Gather natural items from the garden. Flat items produce more detailed prints.
2. Place blueprint paper on top of a piece of cardboard, white side down, blue side up.
3. Arrange natural items on top of the blueprint paper, on the blue side.
4. On top of the arrangement, lay a piece of plexiglas and using clothespins fasten the four layers (cardboard, blueprint paper, natural items, plexiglas) together around the edges.
5. Expose the top of the arrangement (blue side of paper) to the light source—either sun or an overhead projector. Expose until visible paper has lost most of its color.
6. Separate layers and rinse blueprint paper in water to "fix" the print.
7. Dry prints in a flat position.

Tip:
*If you cannot find blueprint paper that can be "fixed" in water, yellow blueprint paper can be "fixed" in a pan of water mixed with ammonia. Add 2 capfuls of ammonia to every 2 cups of water.

87

Brewing Solar Mint Tea (3)

You need fresh mint leaves for this project, so grow some first or get leaves from neighbors who have it.

Things you need:
    *One big handful of mint leaves
    *A two-quart glass jar
    *Water
    *Aluminum foil
    *Honey and ice (optional)
    *Cups

What to do:
1. Fill the jar with water and add a big handful of mint leaves to the jar. Then cover the mouth of the jar with aluminum foil.
2. Let the jar sit in a sunny spot for two or three hours. Then pour a cup of solar mint tea for yourself and each of your friends.
3. Add some ice and honey if you wish.

Mint is easy to grow and does well in partial shade.

Catch the Raccoon's Tail (3)

Catching the raccoon's tail is a great game to play to help vent some of the frustration felt when pests eat the vegetables, and even if raccoons don't get your corn, it's still fun.

What to do:
1. Have the students stand in a line behind the leader, holding each other firmly at the waist. The leader is the raccoon's head and the last person in line becomes the raccoon's tail.
2. A scarf or hanky should be inserted in the last person's back pocket.
3. The head of the raccoon tries to catch its tail (the scarf) and the tail tries to keep away from the head. The tail is caught when the head pulls the scarf or hanky from the pocket.

Source: adapted from "New Games"
New Games Foundation, P.O. Box 7901
San Francisco, California 94120

1 = anytime 2 = before outdoor planting 3 = during the growing season 4 = after the growing season

88

Fish is good fertilizer but it must be covered by plenty of soil.

Plant Corn, Beans, and Squash in a Mound (3)

American Indians planted "the three sisters"—corn, pole beans, and squash—together in a mound. Under each mound they usually placed a dead fish. Children enjoy copying this Indian technique, especially if they paint their faces with water-based face paint and make up stories about the three sisters at the time of planting. Points to discuss at planting time might include:

What did Indians eat?
Where did corn, beans, and squash originally come from?
What happens to the dead fish buried underneath the seeds?
The space-saving value of interplanting. Pole beans will climb the corn stalks and a vining variety of squash will spread out around the mounds.

Things you need:
*Corn, pole bean, and vine squash seeds
*One whole fresh or frozen fish for each mound to be planted
*Prepared garden area

What to do:
1. Dig a shallow hole and bury the fish under 4 or 5 inches of soil. Then plant several seeds of each vegetable about 2 inches apart in a low mound. You may want to thin out some plants later for best growing results.

At Mallets Bay School in Colchester, Vermont, teachers and students paint their faces for this activity.

1 = anytime 2 = before outdoor planting 3 = during the growing season 4 = after the growing season

Making a Solar Food Dryer (3)

This dryer can be built quickly and easily. Children can construct it, and once it is made, they can conduct all sorts of experiments with drying various vegetables and fruits.

Things you need:
  *A cardboard box with dimensions that will leave about 8 inches in front when a 45-degree angle is cut from the top corner.
  *Either black construction paper and glue, or shellac and flat black paint
  *Heavy tape
  *Three or four hangers, straightened out
  *Nylon flyscreen, cut a few inches larger than the bottom of the box
  *A heavy needle and light string to lace the screen onto the box
  *Saran wrap or clear vinyl

What to do:
  1. Cut a 45-degree angle section off from the top of the box as shown. Blacken the entire inside of the box with either black construction paper, or a layer of shellac (let it dry five to seven hours) followed by flat black paint.
  2. Cut a door in the back of the box large enough to let your hand through plus whatever you will be putting in to dry. Reinforce the folded hinging area with heavy tape.
  3. Poke holes with a sharp pencil in the bottom and sides of the box.
  4. Make support wires from the coat hangers by sticking them through the box 6-8 inches up from the bottom, and bending down the ends.
  5. Place the screen on the supports, turning up the extra materials at the sides so that the screening can be laced to the box. Lace the screen to the box with needle and string.
  6. Cover the top of the box with Saran wrap or clear vinyl and secure it with tape.
  7. Make two legs out of cardboard and fasten them to the bottom with heavy tape.

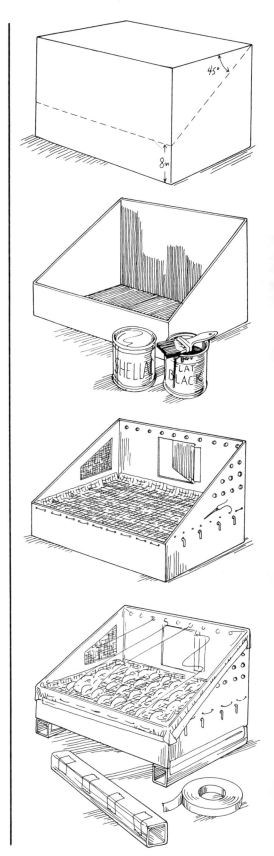

Source: "Connections: A Curriculum in Appropriate Technology for Fifth and Sixth Graders"
National Center for Appropriate Technology
Butte, Montana

1 = anytime 2 = before outdoor planting 3 = during the growing season 4 = after the growing season

A Little Care for Your Tools (3)

Your tools, if properly maintained, will last longer and work better.

Things you need:
*Common mill file
*Bench vise
*Box with sand and old oil
*Linseed or tung oil

What to do:
1. Cleaning: Scrape away all dirt with a wire or scrub brush. Metal parts should be oiled and wiped clean to prevent rust. A good way to clean your tools after use is to plunge them several times into a box filled with sand and old oil. This will clean and oil them at the same time. Straighten out any bent teeth on forks or rakes.
2. Handles: To increase the life and flexibility, sand lightly and treat with linseed or tung oil.
3. Sharpening: Shovels, spades and hoes should have a keen edge. To sharpen, secure tool in a vice or hold securely. Take a good look at the cutting edge and with a common mill file, push across the beveled edge away from you while also sliding it slightly sideways. When blade has a good edge, give the other side of the blade a few light strokes. Oil edge when done.

Making "Manure Tea" Fertilizer (2) (3)

Making liquid fertilizer is a good project for kids. "Manure tea" for plants is made by dropping an old grain bag full of dried or fresh manure into a large bucket of water and "steeping" it for a few days.

Things you need:
*Fresh or dried manure
*Old grain bag
*Large bucket

What to do:
1. Put a few shovelsful of manure into the grain bag.
2. Drop the bag into a large bucket of water. Put a close-fitting cover over the top to keep out flies. Give the brew a stir or two every day until the water is very dark.
3. You may want to dilute the tea somewhat, especially if you are watering very young seedlings with it.
4. When you're finished brewing, empty the bag. Put residue on the compost pile or around plants to mulch them.

1 = anytime 2 = before outdoor planting 3 = during the growing season 4 = after the growing season

Keeping Growth Charts (3)

This is a useful project for record-keeping in the garden. It will help children see the growth process.

Things you need:
    *Notebook and pencil
    *Graph paper
    *Ruler

What to do:
1. Have each gardener measure a plant that will grow fairly upright. Each child should take weekly measurments of the plant's height from germination until harvest, and record this in a notebook.
2. At the end of the season, compile a graph of the data. Put the number of days or weeks on the horizontal x-axis, and inches of growth on the vertical y-axis.
3. Have the children compare their growth rates, and discuss why some plants have grown more than others.

You can also have the children chart their data for inches of rainfall in each week on the same graph, and see if this has a relationship to plant growth.

The Rain Gauge (3)

If you keep weather records for your garden, this is a useful tool. It can also be used to tell if the garden needs watering.

Things you need:
    *A tin can
    *Ruler
    *A crayon or waterproof marker

What to do:
1. With a ruler, measure and mark half-inch or quarter-inch increments up from the bottom inside the can.
2. Put the can out in your garden, and check it regularly. If within a week rain doesn't add up to the 1-inch mark, then your garden needs watering. Dump out the water to record next week's rainfall.

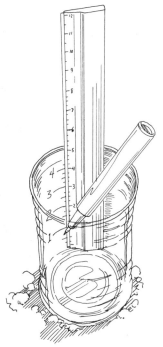

Use rain gauge when watering, too.

1 = anytime 2 = before outdoor planting 3 = during the growing season 4 = after the growing season

92

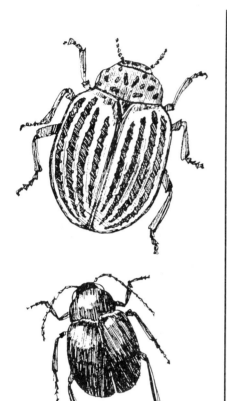

Homemade Insect Spray (3)

Many gardeners use homemade sprays to keep insect pests out of the garden. Test the following garlic-pepper recipe for protection against cabbage worms, caterpillars, tomato hornworms, aphids and other pesky insects.

Things you need:
*Six cloves of garlic, crushed
*One onion, minced
*1 tablespoon dried hot pepper
*1 teaspoon pure soap (not detergent)
*1 gallon hot water

What to do:
1. Blend garlic, onion, pepper and soap in hot water and let the mixture sit for a day or two.
2. Strain before using as a spray.

Tips:
*Water is the carrier, soap makes the spray stick and the plant juices are the active ingredients.
*When using soap, Naphtha is recommended. It will dissolve easily if you add 4 teaspoons of alcohol to a gallon of water.

Garden Skits and Charades (3)

The garden is a perfect stage, props included, for children to make up and perform skits about gardening. This fun project can reinforce important garden concepts.

Things you need:
*Basic tools to put costumes together, such as string, safety pins, tin foil, crepe paper, etc.

What to do:
1. Divide the children into groups of no more than seven. Each group will create their own skit and then perform it. Charades work well, because they require the audience to participate as well as the actors.
2. Write various themes of skits down on scraps of paper and have each group draw a theme from a hat to act out. Themes can be as simple as "thinning," "raccoon eating corn," "planting seeds," or "birds eating worms from the garden."
3. Instead of putting themes in a hat, you can put "characters" or names of garden objects in the hat. Each person draws a character or an object, and the group must develop a skit with a gardening theme around these.
4. Have the children make props and costumes from objects found in the garden.

1 = anytime 2 = before outdoor planting 3 = during the growing season 4 = after the growing season

Raising Worms (3)

Worms are important creatures in a garden. They aerate the soil and help improve its fertility and texture. Learning about worms helps children understand the interdependence of plants and garden organisms.

Things you need:
*Large cardboard box lined with a garbage bag
*Garden soil
*Organic matter and manure
*Starter worms (look for 'red' worms, possibly at a fishing tackle store)
*Screen or other cover to keep out predators

What to do:
1. Put the box in a shady spot, and fill with a mixture of loose soil mixed with organic matter and manure, to about 2 inches below the top of the box. Moisten, and allow it to compost for a few days.
2. Stir up the soil and add the worms. Stir the worm culture every two weeks, keeping it moist at all times, but not wet. Continue to add compost and other organic matter regularly.
3. Add some of the worm culture to your garden every month, making sure you have left enough worms behind in the worm bed to re-produce. If the soil in your garden is fertile, the worms will thrive there.

Tips:
*When turning the worm bed, use a spading fork—the blade of a shovel will cut the worms.
*Worms like rotted straw in their box if you can find some.

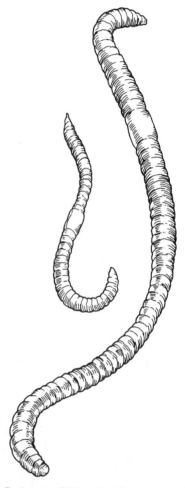

Red worms (left) are best for worm growing project.

1 = anytime 2 = before outdoor planting 3 = during the growing season 4 = after the growing season

94

Vegetable Designs (3)

When cut in half, every vegetable has a different pattern of shapes and textures. Printing is a good way for children to see these patterns, and with experience they can make beautiful decorations and cards.

Things you need:
*Knife
*Vegetables from the garden
*Poster paints or ink pads
*Paper
*A paper plate

What to do:
1. Pour paint onto the plate and spread it evenly.
2. Cut the vegetables in half, and press the cutside into the paint.
3. Lift the vegetable from the paint and press it onto a blank sheet of paper. Be sure not to move the vegetable as you print.
4. Carefully lift the vegetable.

Tips:
*If using ink pads, cut the vegetables and use them like stamps.
*Too much paint on the vegetables will result in a blurred print. For more detail use little paint.

Sensory Awareness (3)

So often we take our sense of sight for granted. We look without seeing. Blindfolds help us learn to "see" what we are looking at.

This exercise also builds trust between partners.

Things you need:
*Blindfolds

What to do:
1. Each pair of students should receive a blindfold.
2. Have them take turns guiding their blind partners through the garden. The guide should help his or her partner explore the plants through the senses of taste, touch, and smell: "Feel this leaf. What plant did it come from? Taste this vegetable and tell me what you are eating."
3. Crush tomato leaves in your fingers—can the blindfolded children tell which plant they belong to? If not, lead them to the tomatoes and have them feel the plant. Now they can guess. With encouragement, children's imaginations run wild in this game, and the guides are sure to think up new ways of testing the senses.

1 = anytime 2 = before outdoor planting 3 = during the growing season 4 = after the growing season

Concentration (3)

This game encourages good coordination, quick thinking, and learning the names of things in the garden.

What to do:
1. Have the children sit cross-legged in a circle. Together, everyone claps their hands twice, hits their legs twice, snaps their right finger, and then snaps their left finger, continuing until a rhythm is developed. At the beginning of the game the rhythms should be slow, and the speed can increase as the children gain in skill.
2. One person begins the verbal part of the game while the rest continue clapping. The speaker, also clapping, says, "Concentration is the name of the game, and kinds of vegetables we will name." The speaker then names a vegetable, and this must be done within the finger-snapping section of the rhythm.
3. Everyone keeps clapping, and moving clockwise around the circle, each person follows in turn by naming a vegetable. No vegetable should be repeated. Repeaters, or one who doesn't add a name while snapping, are "out" of the naming part of the game, but stay in the circle to help with the clapping part. Continue around and around the circle until one person cannot name a vegetable not previously called.
4. Themes can be altered according to the skills of participants, for example, bugs in the garden, flowers in the garden, root crops in the garden, and so on.

1 = anytime 2 = before outdoor planting 3 = during the growing season 4 = after the growing season

Dandelion

Lambs Quarter

Purslane

Weed Salads (3)

For beginning gardeners, it is often difficult to tell young weeds from young garden seedlings. This activity helps reinforce lessons on weeding.

Common weeds that are edible include: pigweed, mustard, purslane, lambs quarter, and dandelion greens.

What to do:

1. Have the children weed their gardens and save the weeds as they work. Work as a group to identify the weeds.
2. Once the weeds have been identified point out which weeds are edible, and the importance of eating only those weeds that you determine are edible.
3. Using the edible weeds and young salad greens and radishes from the garden, make an edible weed salad—and eat it!

Tip:

*It's good to learn about weeds which are toxic, too. Valuable resources for identifying weeds and learning which ones are edible, include:

Eat the Weeds, by Ben C. Harris. Keats Publishing, Inc., 36 Grove Street, P.O. Box 876, New Canaan, CT 06840. $1.50.

Common Weeds of the United States, by the U.S. Department of Agriculture. Dover Publications, Inc., 180 Varick St., New York, NY 10014. $8.95.

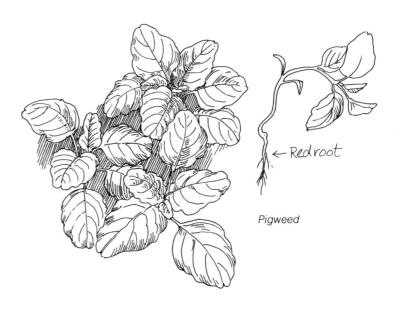

← Redroot

Pigweed

1 = anytime 2 = before outdoor planting 3 = during the growing season 4 = after the growing season

Collecting Insects from Your Garden (3)

Collecting insects is a great thrill for children. You can collect them to look at, and then let them go, or you can collect them for the purpose of developing a permanent collection. In either case, the objective of collecting insects should be educational, with respect for life.

Through insect studies children understand predatory-prey relationships, the concepts of pest management, and the impact of insect life on earth. The main tool you will need for collecting is a net. Each child can make his or her own.

Things you need:

*A wooden handle, 3 feet long (a broom handle or a ¾-inch wooden dowel)
*4 feet of heavy wire (about ⅛-inch in diameter)
*Netting or muslin, a piece 30-inches by 48-inches
*Soft wire or strong tape to wrap around the handle and hoop wire.
*Needle and heavy thread
*Electric drill
*Scissors

What to do:

1. Drill angled holes in the wooden handle large enough for heavy wire to be inserted.
2. Bend the heavy wire to form a hoop, leaving 2 inches on each end to be inserted into holes of wooden handle. Insert wire into holes and bend as indicated.
3. Wrap soft wire or tape around handle to secure the hoop ends.
4. Fold the fabric in half, along the 48-inch dimension, so it measures 24 inches by 30 inches. Cut the cloth in a cone shape with a rounded end.
5. Pin the cut edges together to hold them while you sew the net. Fasten the open end of the net to the wire hoop by folding over the wire and sewing with heavy thread.

Tips:

*"Bug boxes," 1-inch-square boxes with a magnifying glass as a lid, are inexpensive and helpful in getting a better look at insects.
*To make a permanent insect collection, children need to be instructed on techniques of killing, pinning and labeling the insects. A helpful source for this is: *Exploring the Insect World,* by Margaret J. Anderson. McGraw-Hill Book Co., 1221 Avenue of the Americas, New York, NY 10020. $6.95.
*A good book for the identification of common insects is: *Golden Guide to Insects,* by Herbert S. Zim and Clarence Cottam. Golden Press, Dept. M, Western Publishing Co., Inc., 1220 Mound Ave., Racine, WI 53404. $2.95.

Source: Project ROOTS
Lansing, Michigan

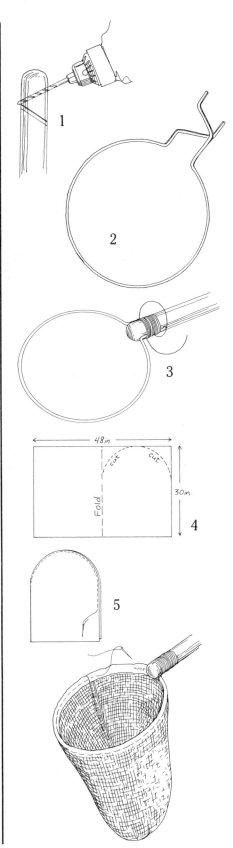

1 = anytime 2 = before outdoor planting 3 = during the growing season 4 = after the growing season

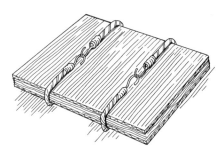

Making a Plant Press (3)

Plant presses are handy tools for garden studies and crafts. Children enjoy pressing garden and weed flowers and later using them to make floral stationery.

Presses can also be used for related botany studies in the garden. Children can collect different weeds (roots and all), identify them, press them, and later mount them on paper or in a garden journal.

There are many ways to make a plant press. Here's one.

Things you need:

*Two sturdy sheets of corrugated cardboard—at least 12 by 12 inches
*Sheets of newspaper or smooth paper toweling
*Two Bungee cords (fabric-coated elastic cord with metal hooks at both ends, commonly sold at sporting goods stores) or heavy string.

What to do:

1. Have each of the children take the materials needed for his or her own press to the garden to collect weeds and flowers.
2. Arrange each plant on a layer of several sheets of newspaper or toweling, far enough apart so that the specimens will not touch each other.
3. When the first layer is filled, place several more sheets of paper on top of it, and start a new layer.
4. Continue in this way, finishing with a layer of papers, then enclose this all between the pieces of cardboard and secure it with string or Bungee cords.
5. Allow plants to dry three to four days. It helps to lay the press under a heavy stack of books or magazines. If the plants are not completely dry in this time, disassemble the press, replace the papers, and tie it back together, putting it under the weight again for another three days.

Tips:

*Make sure that thick and thin types of plants are not on the same layer—that would make them press unevenly.
*Use all parts of the plants, not just flowers.
*It is better to cut rather than pick the plants.
*After pressing, sometimes flowers fade. Touching them up later with watercolor paints is fun.
*To mount pressed plants on paper, use spots of glue applied with the point of a toothpick.
*Children like to decorate the cover of their plant presses with their own pressed plants. A layer of clear plastic spray or shellac will make them more durable. Have children learn where shellac comes from, too.
*Useful books for identification with color photographs are: *Common Weeds of the United States,* by the U.S. Department of Agriculture. Dover Publications, Inc., 180 Varick St., New York, NY 10014. $8.95. *Weeds,* by Alexander C. Martin (Golden Guide Series). Western Publishing Co., Inc. Orders to: Dept. M, 1220 Mound Ave., Racine, WI 53404. $2.95

1 = anytime 2 = before outdoor planting 3 = during the growing season 4 = after the growing season

Bean Thrashing (3) (1)

This is a very active way to learn about dried beans.

Things you need:
   *Mature, dried bean plants with pods
   *Grain sacks
   *3-4 foot tree branch about 2 inches in diameter
   *Blanket
   *String

What to do:
   1. Fill the grain sacks with dried bean plants and pods. Then tie the bags closed.
   2. Let the children very carefully beat the grain bags with the branches. (A safer way is to ask kids to jump on the sack.) Once the beans are knocked out of pods, pull out large plant parts from the sacks.
   3. Pour the remaining contents onto a blanket.
   4. Have the children circle around the blanket, grab hold of the edges and gently toss the blanket up and down without letting go. The branches, stems and pods will blow away or separate from the beans.
   5. Split the harvest up among the kids, make soup or save the beans to plant next year.

Empty pods are pulled out of grain sack after kids beat on the sacks.

1 = anytime 2 = before outdoor planting 3 = during the growing season 4 = after the growing season

100

Bird Feeders (3) (1)

Birds are important garden life, and making bird feeders is a great craft project. Bird feeders should be located in areas protected from bad weather. The open side of the feeder should be placed away from the wind. This protects the food when the birds might need it most.

Shrubs and trees help protect bird feeders from the weather. They also provide the birds with shelter and protection from their predators.

To discover what foods are favorites among birds in your neighborhood, divide a feeding tray into six compartments, and place a different type of food in each compartment. Experiment with corn, sunflower seeds, peanuts, suet, rice, and bread crumbs. At first, only offer small amounts of each food type. You can give the birds more of certain foods as they select their favorites.

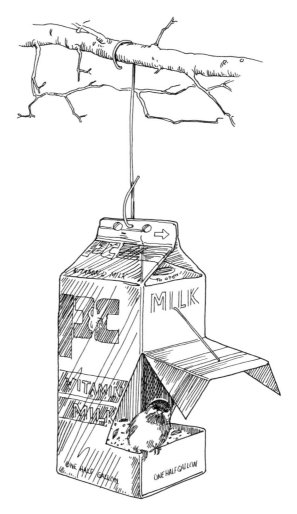

Crafting a Corn Husk Doll (3) (1)

The Indians were the first to make corn husk dolls. Corn husks were dried, tied, and fashioned into squaws, chiefs, and braves. Faces were painted, and sticks were used to make arms and sometimes legs.

The doll design here is created with yarn and corn husks which, when properly tied, produce all body parts. Use other materials to create clothing, and attach facial features with glue.

Things you need:
   *12 corn husks
   *Yarn, string or cord
   *Scissors

What to do:
1. Gather 12 corn husks from garden corn and tie them tightly together at one end with yarn or string.
2. To make the head, tie the husks a little way down from the top knot.
3. Gather three of the husks, and tie them together halfway down for an arm. Gather and tie three more husks, at the opposite side of the doll to form another arm. Cut away most of the excess corn husk that is below the knots.
4. To make the body, tie the remaining corn husks halfway between the head and their ends.
5. Make the legs by taking three husks and tying them together a little up from their ends.
6. Make the other leg the same way.
7. Decorate with colored felt-tip markers, construction paper, fabric, or any other craft supplies you may have.

*Source: "Snips and Snails &
Walnut Whales"
Workman Publishing,
New York, N.Y.*

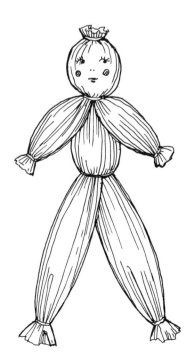

1 = anytime 2 = before outdoor planting 3 = during the growing season 4 = after the growing season

Corn Grinding and Patty Making (3) (1)

This is a two-part project: grinding corn into meal and then making corn patties and cooking them.

Things you need for corn grinding:
*Dried corn for grinding, either flint corn or Indian corn. You can grow the corn in the school garden (the previous year) or purchase dried corn from a food co-op or health food store.
*Grinding logs, made by carving out the end of a log (log size approximately 14 inches in diameter and 1-2 feet long) to make a shallow bowl.
*Smooth, hard rocks for grinding. They should be small enough for the children to hold easily, but large enough to crush the corn.

What to do:
1. Set the log in a vertical position with the bowl end up.
2. Place a handful of corn in the bowl and grind, grind, grind. Some of the corn will fly off the log but that's okay.
3. Have students grind until they get at least a quarter of a cup of corn meal each.

Things you need for patty making:
*Ground corn
*Fire or heat source for cooking
*Honey
*Cooking oil, bowl, and spoon
*Spatula
*Frying pan, griddle or sheet of slate

What to do:
1. Mix corn meal and honey in a bowl. Use enough honey to make the dough stick together.
2. Shape patties by pressing the dough between the palms of your hands.
3. Oil the cooking surface and brown patties on both sides.
4. You can cook the patties in a frying pan or griddle or on a stove top, or better yet, on slate placed over a bed of campfire coals.

1 = anytime 2 = before outdoor planting 3 = during the growing season 4 = after the growing season

A Dazzling Carrot Necklace! (3) (1)

Carrots are good tasting, good for you, and good-looking around your neck!

Things you need:
    *Carrots
    *Heavy thread
    *Darning needle
    *Knife

What to do:
1. Wash the carrots and then slice them about ¼-inch thick.
2. Thread your needle (thread should be long enough to go around head plus some extra) and then slip the carrot slices onto the thread by pushing the needle into the center of each slice.
3. Once you have strung enough carrots to go around your head, tie the ends together to form a necklace.
4. Lay your necklace on a piece of paper in a dark place to dry, making sure none of the carrots touch each other. As the carrots harden and dry, they turn into wrinkled beads. The drying process takes about a week.

Youngster wearing fresh carrot necklace before "carrot beads" are dry.

Making Veggie Creatures (3) (1)

Constructing animals out of vegetables works best when designs are left to the kids. Veggie creatures make great decorations for harvest parties, or for children to take home and display.

Things you need:
    *Vegetables and flowers from the garden
    *Knife
    *Round toothpicks

What to do:
Give the kids encouragement and see what they produce. Use the toothpicks to stick veggies together. You can use either whole vegetables or cut up pieces to add appendages, eyes, ears, tails, and so on.

1 = anytime 2 = before outdoor planting 3 = during the growing season 4 = after the growing season

Dry flowers upside down in warm, dark room.

Drying Flowers (3) (1)

Capturing the color and beauty of the summer garden for display in winter is easy and rewarding. Include in your garden varieties of flowers that are easily air dried. The flowers and seed pods of garden annuals and perennials, along with flowers, grasses, and seed pods found in the wild, provide endless sources of plant materials for flower arrangements, bouquets, and wreaths.

Here is a selection of plants to choose from. Seeds can be ordered through seed catalogs. Most all flowers for drying need to be started indoors and transplanted into the garden, so plan ahead.

Annuals
Acroclinium (*Acroclinium helipterum*)
Bells of Ireland (*Molucella Laevis*)
Celosia (*Celosia argentea*)
Globe Amaranth (*Gomphrena globosa*)
Love-in-a-Mist (pods) (*Nigella*)
Poppy (pods) (*Papaver*)
Starflower (*Scabios stellata*)
Statice (*Limonium sinuatum*)
Strawflower (*Helichrysum*)
Xeranthemum

Perennials
Baby's Breath (double variety) (*Gypsophila paniculata*)
Columbine (pods) (*Aquilegia*)
Globe Thistle (*Echinops ritro*)
Statice (perennial) (*Limonium latifolium, Limonium caspia*)
Tansy (*Tanacetum vulgare*)
Yarrow (*Achillea millefolium*)

Wildflowers that air-dry easily (not to be planted in garden)
Dock (*Rumex crispus*)
Goldenrod (*Solidago species*)
Joe-Pye Weed (*Eupatorium purpureum*)
Pearly Everlasting (*Anaphalis margaretacea*)
Queen Anne's Lace (*Daucus carota*)
Rabbit's Foot Clover (*Trifolium arvense*)
Steeplebush (hardhack) (*Spirea tomentosum*)

Look for other seed pods, grasses and other flowers.

Things you need:
*Plant material
*String
*Rubber bands
*20-gauge straight floral wire (available at florists and hobby shops)
*Floral tape (available at florists and hobby shops)
*Scissors

1 = anytime 2 = before outdoor planting 3 = during the growing season 4 = after the growing season

What to do:
1. A general rule—pick all flowers before they are fully developed.
2. Remove foliage from flower stem.
3. Group flowers into small bunches and tie them together firmly with string or a rubber band. If using string, leave enough on the end to make a hanging loop.
4. Hang flower bunches in a dry, warm, dark, airy location. (Damp, cool areas encourage mold and mildew.) The length of drying time will vary depending on weather conditions and the amount of moisture in the plants. Keep checking!
5. Some of the plants listed have weak stems and will need the support of a wire stem in order to be used.
6. To attach flower to wire, cut stem of flower, leaving about 2 inches. Holding the stem and the wire next to each other, wind floral tape around them both. Stretch and press the tape firmly as you wind it. Tear off the end of the tape and pinch it tightly around the wire stem.

Tips:
*To make flower arrangements, decorate the outside of clean half-pint milk cartons with construction paper. Fill the containers with sand and arrange flowers by placing natural and wire stems directly in the sand.

*If you want to store the dried plant materials before using them, pack them lightly into cardboard boxes.

Good resources are:

The Dried Flower Book by Annette Mierhof. E.P. Dutton, Elsevier-Dutton Publishing Co., Inc., 2 Park Avenue, New York, NY 10016. $14.50.

Botanical Wreaths by Rachel C. Hartley & Jane B. Holliday. Flower Press Publishers.

106

Grinding Wheat Berries into Flour (1)

Children love to turn the handle of a mill and watch how flour is made. Borrow a mill or ask the local tool stores if they will let you rent one for an afternoon.

Things you need:
*Stalks of wheat
*3-4 cups of wheat berries
*Two medium mixing bowls
*Pictures of wheat fields
*Lots of small jars with lids
*Flour mill

What to do:
1. Find a suitable place for using a hand-powered grain mill.
2. Examine stalks of wheat (if available), a handful of wheat berries, pictures of wheat fields, and a loaf of bread.
3. Each person should turn the handle of the mill for a while, feeling the tension of the machine, hearing the sound of grinding, smelling, and tasting the texture of the flour.
4. Talk about the transformation of wheat berries to bread. Count the number of participants who want a stash of flour and divide the flour until everyone has a share.
5. While taking the mill apart, discuss what can be done with fresh flour and when. Options are baking a loaf of bread, making finger-paint or flour-on-glue pictures, or papier mache, etc.

Tip:

To expand the lesson, include grinding peanuts, soybeans, and rice. Or take the time to mix and knead a batch of bread dough. Sculpt the dough or bake a loaf. Treat another group with home made bread and peanut butter. Draw pictures of fields of wheat, a machine to grind food, a loaf of bread you would bake for a friend. Find the word "wheat" in the dictionary and in the encyclopedia.

*Source: "Edible City
Resource Manual"
William Kaufman, Inc.
Los Altos, California*

107

Learning about Seed Production (1)

Children should understand the full cycle of a plant's life, and this means knowing what happens from germination all the way to the time when the plant produces its own seed.

Things you need:

   *A leafy vegetable, such as lettuce or spinach which you allow to go to seed.

What to do:

   Tell the children that you are allowing certain plants to go to seed, and have them observe the processes of flowering seed production, and the natural scattering of the seeds. Save some of the seeds for next year, but remember that hybrid varieties may produce a different plant the next season. Save seeds of other plants as well, such as flowers.

Tips:

   *If you save the seeds for next year, keep them in a very dry, airtight, dark container. Film canisters work well. Store them in a refrigerator or freezer.

   *A delightful story to read during your discussion of seeds and life cycles is *The Pumpkin People,* by David and Maggie Cavagnaro, published by Charles Scribner's Sons, 597 Fifth Ave., New York, NY 10017.

Many greens will go to seed in warm weather.

1 = anytime 2 = before outdoor planting 3 = during the growing season 4 = after the growing season

108

Sing a Song

Singing is a perfect activity for kids gardening and David Mallett's "Garden Song" is a catchy, happy, absolutely delightful tune which kids love to sing. (We've even heard kids sing it while weeding.) Both Mallett and Pete Seeger have recorded it in recent years so look for their albums to hear the zest and feeling they put into the words.

First verse and chorus:
Inch by inch, row by row,
Gonna make this garden grow,
All it takes is a rake and a hoe
And a piece of fertile ground.
Inch by inch, row by row,
Someone bless these seeds I sow,
Someone warm them from below
'Til the rain comes tumblin' down.

Second verse:
Pullin' weeds and pickin' stones,
Man is made of dreams and bones,*
Feel the need to grow my own
'Cause the time is close at hand.
Grain for grain, sun and rain,
Find my way in nature's chain,
Tune my body and my brain
To the music from the land. (Chorus)

Third verse:
Plant your rows straight and long,
Temper them with prayer and song,**
Mother Earth will make you strong
If you give her love and care.
Old crow watching hungrily,
From his perch in yonder tree,
In my garden I'm as free
As that feathered thief up there. (Chorus)

Garden Song
by David Mallett

*Seeger suggests singing "We are made..." instead of original "Man is made..."
**Seeger also suggests "Plant your rows short or long/Season with with a cheerful song" instead of the original words here.

© Copyright 1975 Cherry Lane Music Co.
This arrangement © Copyright 1979 Cherry Lane Music Co.
International Copyright Secured All Rights Reserved

1 = anytime 2 = before outdoor planting 3 = during the growing season 4 = after the growing season

Some other activity suggestions

*Writing haiku and cinquain poetry on garden topics
*Publishing a class newspaper about the garden
*Writing to pen pals in other school or youth garden programs
*Creating a garden game complete with a gameboard and rules
*Producing a photo exhibit, slide show or video about your garden

*Comparing the cost of produce in markets to home-grown produce
*Taking garden produce to the local food pantry or soup kitchen
*Collecting and discussing newspaper articles that deal with the
 food industry, hunger, nutrition and agriculture
*Studying about and growing specific ethnic foods
*Studying about the contribution of Native American foods to our
 agriculture and diet
*Investigating how magazine ads influence our food choices

*Sprouting an avocado seed, carrot or pineapple top, celery stalk
 or sweet potato
*Building an enclosed terrarium to demonstrate the water cycle
*Charting daily temperatures in Fahrenheit and Celcius

*Taking a field trip to a farm, market stand, apiary, arboretum, etc.
*Comparing the taste of garden-ripened tomatoes with green or
 store bought tomatoes
*Canning and freezing fruits and vegetables

*Braiding onions and garlic for gifts
*Making herbal vinegars and sachets
*Making a garden scarecrow
*Constructing mobiles with garden materials, pine cones, sticks of
 wood, etc.
*Making carrot juice
*Doing still-life paintings of produce and flowers

    The following activities which were described in this chapter were
adapted from *A Basic Curriculum Guide for School Gardens,* prepared by
Dianne L. Peterson, Youth Gardens Coordinator, and published by the Uni-
versity of California Cooperative Extension Service: Children, Gardens and
Poetry; Garden Riddles; Naming the Biggest, Smallest and Most Interesting;
Keeping Growth Charts; Vegetable Designs; A Dazzling Carrot Necklace;
Learning About Seed Production.

6

THE BASICS OF INDOOR GARDENING & CONTAINER GARDENING

"We want children to learn that a food chain is not a string of supermarkets, but a process of producing nutritious food—and that they can be part of the process by learning how to plan, plant, harvest and preserve their own food."

*Kathryn Berhnoft and Pam Erickson,
Garden Instructors
Project Sow and Save
Sequim, Washington*

INDOOR GARDENING TECHNIQUES

A good way to stretch a garden program with kids or to have a program when an outdoor garden is not feasible is to involve them in growing plants indoors. Many programs raise seedlings indoors for later transplanting to the outdoor garden while others grow abundant gardens and raise plants to maturity indoors. It takes planning, a little special know-how and some restraint at seeding time to create a smooth indoor-growing operation. A common mistake is to have too many flats and pots sprouting vegetables. Caring for them over time may become a big burden.

The basics of indoor growing—and a few fine points—are presented in this chapter. Good gardening books will have additional helpful information.

Transplant Chart

If you are raising seedlings for your outdoor garden, fill in the last average frost date for your area. Count back and start your seeds.

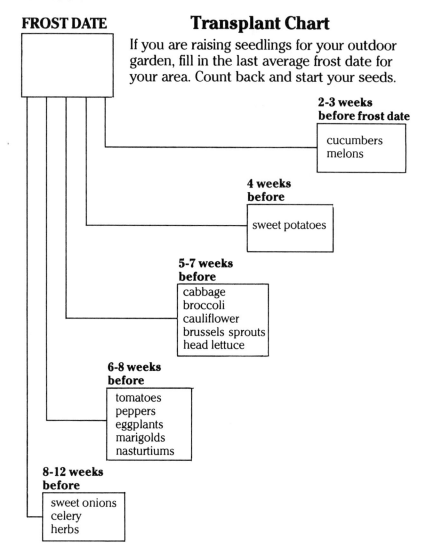

FROST DATE

2-3 weeks before frost date

cucumbers
melons

4 weeks before

sweet potatoes

5-7 weeks before

cabbage
broccoli
cauliflower
brussels sprouts
head lettuce

6-8 weeks before

tomatoes
peppers
eggplants
marigolds
nasturtiums

8-12 weeks before

sweet onions
celery
herbs

112

Keep fluorescent lights close to seedlings.

A small system for growing seedlings under lights

Put plant trays on ⅜- to ½-inch thick plywood, supported by sawhorses. Light fixtures should be adjustable up and down because bulbs should be 3-6 inches from plants at all times for best growth. If you can't adjust lights, use pieces of wood to raise flats and trays close to lights and lower them later as plants grow. You should also rotate your trays because the light is strongest near the center of the table.

Ordinary cool-white (40 watt) fluorescent bulbs and standard fixtures are fine. Higher-priced "grow lights" are designed for flowering houseplants.

Use one pair of bulbs for every 1-foot width of growing area. Length of available bulbs and fixtures will vary from store to store. Discount stores occasionally offer low-priced "shop light" bulbs and fixtures which, although bulky, are excellent lights for young vegetable seedlings.

Lights should ideally be on for 16 hours a day, but plants can get by with slightly less for short periods. A timer ($9-$20) can regulate power for turning lights on in early morning and off at night.

Pots and trays abound

Almost any container or pot that holds a couple of inches of soil can be used for starting vegetables. There are plenty of possibilities: milk cartons (cut quarts lengthwise, half-gallons and gallons widthwise), dish pans, Styrofoam and paper cups, disposable pie plates, etc. Just be sure to poke a few drainage holes in them before adding soil.

Get a few standard peat pots ($.02-.05 each) and plastic seed-starting trays ($1 or less) to balance your collection.

Use "soil-less" soil

Garden soil tends to be too heavy for good seedling growth and contains disease organisms which cause damping off and seed rot diseases of young seedlings indoors. It can, however, be mixed with sand, vermiculite or other materials to lighten it up and can be pasteurized by heating it in a shallow pan at 200 degrees for 30 minutes or so. (A smelly process!) Soil temperature should reach 160-180 degrees F.

More convenient, although more expensive to use, are soilless growing media, such as Pro Mix, Vita-Earth, Jiffy Mix and others. These mixes are sterilized and present little disease problem. They are light enough for good drainage and root growth yet spongy enough to hold moisture well.

Some mixes have a little extra fertilizer added to them. If you buy the mix by the bale ($12-20), you'll get the most for your money.

One way to stretch the mix is to put ordinary garden soil on the bottom of your flats and pots and to use the mix on the top layers. You'll get good germination of seeds with some protection from diseases.

Germination and right temperature go hand in hand

Soil temperature is very important for quick germination of seeds. Most vegetables will need warm soil to germinate. Peppers, eggplant and tomatoes will be very slow to come up in cool soil. Soil can be kept warm, even in a room that stays cool overnight by keeping flats near heat sources or using heating pads directly under the soil.

NEEDS COOL TO WARM SOIL (50-70 F.)	NEEDS WARM SOIL (70-90 F.)
Broccoli	Pepper
Cabbage	Tomato
Cauliflower	Eggplant
Lettuce	Cucumbers, melons,
Onions	pumpkin and squash
	Corn

Most people start vegetable seeds in late winter, so putting them on the windowsill to germinate is not a good idea. It gets much too cold at night. Put pots and flats where there will be a steady, warm temperature.

Watering

If you place your flats and trays in sealed plastic bags after planting, the soil will stay moist for a while. Be sure to remove the plastic when plants can be seen poking through the soil. After that, be sure to feel the soil often. Press the soil firmly with your fingertips. If it is not moist, water. Plants on a table near a radiator or a heater will dry out quickly. You may have to water daily, especially when the plants are growing fast.

"Bottom watering" is a safe and easy method. Fill a sink or large pan with 2 inches of water; put your flat or pots in until the water seeps up to the surface of the soil. Warning: bottom watering may cause milk cartons and other not-so-sturdy containers to rot or come apart.

Fertilizing

With soil-less growing medium, start fertilizing the plants when they are about an inch tall. Ordinary houseplant food, diluted to the proper concentration, will work fine. Keep a calendar near all your flats and mark in the days when you've added fertilizer to the plants' water. A little bit of plant food once a week is about right for most vegetables.

Bottom watering is quick and doesn't disturb small, tender seedlings.

114

JACK HALE

Best bets for starting and re-potting inside

Lettuce will come up quickly inside and is almost indestructable when being re-potted. Sow seeds thickly in a wide tray or flat and when 1 or 2 inches tall, youngsters can dig them up with a popsicle stick or spoon and replant them 2 or 3 inches apart in separate containers. The root systems of lettuce plants recover very quickly from transplanting, so even those mishandled along the way will probably survive.

Broccoli, cabbage and **cauliflower** will sprout very fast. Keep an eye on them after they are planted and as soon as they come up put them under lights. They get leggy if they don't receive adequate light.

They are fun to transplant to new containers because they respond quickly in their new quarters. Transplant them at least 3 inches from their neighbors in deeper pots or trays.

Onions are a little slower to grow from seed than cabbage and its relatives. However, because the seed is plentiful and inexpensive, it's a good learning crop. Sow flats thickly, and transplant only those onions that are really crowded together, closer than one-half inch. They like deep pots because they usually grow indoors for two months before being planted outside, and thus need room for root development.

Tomatoes, peppers and **eggplants** enjoy growing in deep, roomy pots, though they may be started in a shallow flat and transplanted out when they get their second sets of leaves. In warm soil they should emerge in five to ten days. Tomatoes will develop extra root strength if buried in a deep container up to the top cluster of leaves. You'll have to strip off the lower pairs of leaves first.

Corn is usually planted outside directly in the garden, but it can be transplanted successfully. Youngsters can sow two seeds to a pot about an inch deep. Later, the weaker plant can be pinched out.

Cucumbers, melons, pumpkins and **squash** should be started in individual pots about four weeks before the last expected frost date in spring. However, they do not like re-potting, so just give them plenty of light and sunshine and leave them alone for three weeks. Give them increasing amounts of outdoor time for a week or so and then plant them out in the garden.

Vegetables Suitable for Transplanting and Methods of Sowing Seed

Easy to transplant. Can be sown in flat in rows and transplanted bare root.

Broccoli (5-7)
Brussels sprouts (5-7)
Cabbage (5-7)
Cauliflower (5-7)
Celeriac (7-12)
Celery (7-12)
Chinese Cabbage (5-7)
Collards (5-7)
*Eggplant (6-8)
Lettuce (5-7)
Onion (8-10)
Parsley (8-10)
*Peppers (6-8)
Sweet Potato (3-4)
  (start from tuber
  and not seed)
*Tomato

Must be started in individual containers and transplanted without disturbing roots.

Cantaloupe (3-4)
  (all muskmelons) (3-4)
Cucumbers (3-4)
Squash (3-4)
  (summer & winter)
Watermelon (5-7)

*Sometimes sown in flats and then transplanted into individual containers before transplanting to garden.
( ) Number in parentheses is approximate time (weeks) from sowing seed to transplanting to garden.

Indoor Growing With Greenhouses

More and more youth garden groups are incorporating greenhouses, both for starting seedlings and for year-round growing, into their programs.

But aren't they a large financial investment? Not necessarily. There are many unused or under-used greenhouses that have been claimed by innovative youth leaders. Contact your local school system, parks department, garden center, botanical gardens or university to inquire about utilizing greenhouse space. If you already have or plan to build your own, remember that they do require constant monitoring, but the rewards of greenhouse growing are great. For inspiration and comprehensive information on greenhouse construction and management, consult the greenhouse books in the resource section.

SCHOOLS GROW PLANTS ALL THE WAY TO HARVEST–INDOORS

The Knox Parks Foundation of Hartford, Connecticut, educates people about horticulture, primarily through innovative school gardening programs. The Foundation believes that childhood is the time to learn about gardening; that school is a good place for gardening lessons; that gardening can improve life at school, enhance the curriculum, beautify the buildings and grounds, and provide wonderful opportunities for success and cooperation.

The Foundation's purpose is to expose as many children to gardening as possible, and its "traveling programs" reached too few children with too brief an experience. Therefore, in 1981 the Foundation decided to train teachers to garden with students rather than presenting programs directly to students.

Like many former school gardeners, Hartford teachers faced a short New England growing season and harsh climate, fear of vandalism, lack of nearby growing space, the difficulty of supervising children in the garden and severe pressure on classroom time. In response, with the support of Connecticut Mutual Life Insurance Company and the CIGNA Corporation, the Foundation developed a program of indoor gardening under lights. It allowed teachers and students to grow all sorts

JACK HALE

Hartford school gardeners grow plants indoors.

Young scientists explore plant life cycles in the Grow Lab.

CLEVELAND PUBLIC SCHOOLS

of vegetables, herbs and flowers from seed to maturity right in the classroom.

The heart of the program is the Indoor Growing Center, a 2-foot by 4-foot by 3-foot high frame that allows gardeners to suspend eight fluorescent tubes just above their growing plants. Controlled by a timer, the lights provide as much light as nearly any field vegetables, flowers or herbs require.

Teachers use the indoor gardens in many ways. While giving students the basics of gardening, teachers also supplement and enliven lessons in social sciences, physical sciences, math, language arts, art and most other parts of the curriculum. The gardens spark   interest from teachers, administrators, parents, and, best of all, some of the formerly "unreachable" students.

From a small group of two dozen teachers in the spring of 1982, the program has expanded to include about 150 teachers in nearly every elementary school in Hartford. Upwards of 3,000 students *each year* in every grade from nursery school to 12th grade are experiencing the joy of gardening. An important fact is that very few teachers drop out of the program. Year by year they become not "teachers who garden" but "gardening teachers."

As interest in this type of program has spread, the Knox Parks Foundation has begun, with the support of the Hartford Foundation for Public Giving, to offer training and equipment to school systems and teachers throughout central Connecticut.

National Gardening Association's Grow Lab Program

The National Gardening Association, inspired by the Hartford program, has developed an exciting indoor gardening program called Grow Lab. Interest in Grow Lab is spreading quickly. NGA field-tested Grow Lab programs in dozens of schools and other educational settings nationwide, and found great enthusiasm among teachers and youth leaders. They find the indoor gardens to be easy to manage, relatively inexpensive and not subject to whims of weather, growing season or vandals. They can be established anywhere—in just eight square feet indoors, fruitful gardens grow. Classes come to life as Grow Lab activities are easily integrated with educational objectives.

For further information on curriculum, program or technical information to accompany Grow Lab units write: Grow Lab Program, National Gardening Association, 180 Flynn Avenue, Burlington, Vermont 05401.

WHEN SPACE IS AT A PREMIUM, TRY CONTAINER GARDENING!

Some reasons why it's smart to think about container gardening.

*Containers save space. They need sun, of course, but they can be put anywhere, such as on a concrete sidewalk, next to a building, on balconies, in courtyards, etc.

*Containers save money because most are free. Examples: tires, sewer tiles, chimney flue tiles, baskets, garbage cans, crates, whiskey barrels, nail kegs, metal drums, buckets, plastic pails, bleach jugs, plastic bags, cement blocks.

*Containers can be moved inside at night to protect them from vandalism.

*Kids can take containers home at the end of the school year.

*Container gardening is not overwhelming. It's a good introduction to youth gardening.

*No real soil is needed, as plant growing media (available at most garden centers) can be used. These "soil-less" plant growing materials provide everything but earthworms and the vegetables will grow fine.

JACK HALE

Set up some containers for vertical gardening

Vertical gardening is container gardening with a difference: part of the container is your own wall or fence. Plants grown this way take up almost no ground space.

Take a wooden plank, wrap it with 2-by-2½ inch welded heavy wire mesh to form a half cylinder and staple it securely all around. Fasten the plank to a wall or fence. Pack it with a lining of wet sphagnum moss, in the same way you pack a wire basket. (As a cheaper alternative, use black plastic film because it will quickly be covered by plant growth anyway.)

Prevent water problems by inserting a perforated plastic pipe in the container or a watering cylinder of hardware cloth filled with pebbles. For a wide vertical container use several inserts, placed a foot or so apart. Next, add soil mix, and plant.

Transplants are inserted through the wire and the moss or plastic. For a decorative container use lantana, fuschia, petunias, ivy geraniums, or other flowering plants. They'll all trail down as they grow, and can be pegged down here and there to cover the container completely.

Source: "Money Saving Garden Magic" by Judith Nelson, Prentice-Hall, Inc. Englewood Cliffs, N.J.

Pack Moss & plant up to here

Insert plants all the way up this vertical growing system.

This pillow pak was made by cutting and stapling a thick trash bag.

A "pillow pak" garden needs only sun!

Sausage culture, container culture, and *pillow pak* are a few of the terms used for growing plants in plastic bags (which resemble pillows when filled with soil). Pillow paks need no soil and very little space. Just put them where there's six to eight hours of sun each day.

For your first pillow pak use low-growing vegetables and flowers such as lettuce, dwarf tomatoes, peppers, and petite marigolds or pansies.

1. The medium, a combination of sphagnum peat moss, horticultural vermiculite and fertilizer, can be purchased as a mix. For example Jiffy Mix or Redi Earth in a 4-quart bag will provide enough mix for 15 half-pints.

2. Youths can also mix their own potting medium. For a bushel of mix, use the following formula (T=tablespoon):

   Horticultural vermiculite #2 size . . . . ½ bu
   Peat moss . . . . ½ bu
   Ground limestone . . . . 5 T
   Powdered super-phosphate (0-20-0) . . . . 2 T
   or
   Rock phosphate . . . . 4 T
   4-2-4 fertilizer, preferably organic . . . . 10 T

3. Place the material on a clean surface or in a container and mix thoroughly. Add water until mixture is wet.

4. Pillow paks can be made from heavy polyethylene bags, freezer bags, or garbage bags.

5. Fill the bag with the growing medium until it is moderately firm and then fold and staple the end.

6. Cut holes for the plants at appropriate spots. A 2-gallon plastic bag can accommodate either one dwarf tomato plant, four to six leaf lettuce plants, two pepper plants, six to nine petite marigolds, or four to six pansies.

7. Since there is no drainage in the pak, excessive watering may result in waterlogging of the soil mix and death of the plants. Water only when the medium appears to be dry, usually at one or two week intervals, depending on whether the plants are grown indoors or outdoors.

8. The fertilizer in the pak will support plant growth for about 10 weeks. If plants are grown longer than this, additional feeding may be needed. Feeding can be done by watering with a solution of 2 teaspoons of water-soluble fertilizer per gallon of water.

9. Pillow paks may be placed on a window sill, patio, or porch. If they are planted in the ground, the bottom of the pak should be slit with a knife to allow the root system to penetrate the soil and obtain moisture and nutrients. Use thin bamboo canes to support tall plants.

(Adapted from 4-H Leaders' Guide L-10-10, "Cultural Experiments with Vegetable Crops," by Leonard D. Topoleski, Cooperative Extension Service, Cornell University, N.Y.)

Many things make good containers

Bushel basket with inner liner of plastic

Old bushel baskets—even with holes in the bottom—will grow plenty of food. Use a double layer of plastic trash bags for an inner layer. You don't have to punch drainage holes if you use a soil-less medium and are careful about watering. Add a little fertilizer twice a month to your plants' water.

Note: A solid cardboard box can be used in place of the basket.

Styrofoam coolers as planters

Styrofoam coolers are inexpensive and are excellent plant pots. Poke a few holes in the bottom with a screwdriver and put some gravel or small stones in them to help drainage. One good soil is a mixture of peat moss, commercial potting soil, and a small amount of composted cow manure.

Flue tiles

Cracked or chipped chimney flue tiles make good planters, and you can often get them free from building supply companies. Fill the bottom half of the tiles with leaves or other material, and put soil or a soil-less medium in the top half.

CONTAINER GARDENING GUIDE

PLANT	VARIETY	POT SIZE	PLANTS PER POT
BEANS			
Bush	Tender Crop	6 inch	3-4
	Romano	6 inch	3-4
Pole	Blue Lake	Hanging basket	3-4
BEETS	Ruby Queen	6 inch	4-5
	Burpee's Golden	6 inch	4-5
	Little Ball	6 inch	5-6
BROCCOLI	Italian Sprouting	Bushel basket (tub)	1
	Green Comet	Bushel basket (tub)	1
CABBAGE	Dwarf Morden	Tub, bushel basket	3-4
CUCUMBER	Patio Pik	Hanging basket, tub	1-2
	Pot Luck	Tub	2-3
	Bush Whopper	8-12 inch	1
	Bushcrop	Tub, bushel basket	2
CARROT	Little Finger	6 inch	8-10
	Baby Finger Nantes	6 inch	6-8
	Planet	6 inch	8-10
CELERY	Chinese	6 inch	4-5
CHIVES	Chinese or Daffodil	4 inch	2-3
	Garden Chives	4 inch	2-3
EGGPLANT	Long Tom	6 inch	1
	Classic	6 inch	1
	Morden Midget	6 inch	1
	Japanese Long Purple	6 inch	1
	Slim Jim	6 inch	1
HONEYDEW MELON	Bush Dwarf	Tub	1
LETTUCE	Simpson	6 inch	4-6
	Oakleaf	6 inch	6-10
	Salad Bowl	6 inch	3-4
	Ruby	6 inch	6-10
MUSKMELON	Minnesota Midget	12 inch or bushel basket	1-2
PARSLEY	Flat or Italian	12 inch or bushel basket	3-5
	Triple or Curled	12 inch or bushel basket	3-5
PEAS	Snow Bird	Hanging basket	4-8
Sugar or	Dwarf Gray Sugar	Hanging basket	4-8
Snow	Oregon Sugarpod	Hanging basket	4-8

PLANT	VARIETY	POT SIZE	PLANTS PER POT
HOT PEPPER	Jalapano	10 inch or bushel basket	1-2
	Hungarian Wax	6 inch	1
PEPPER	Yolo Wonder	8 inch	1
	Bell Boy	8 inch	1
	Canape	8 inch	1
	Sweet Banana	8 inch	1
RADISH	Champion	6 inch	6-8
	Cherry Bell	6 inch	6-8
SPINACH	New Zealand	8 inch hanging basket	3-4
	Melody Hybrid	6 inch hanging basket	4-6
SQUASH	Butterbush	Bushel basket	1
	Table King	Bushel basket	1
	Zucchini	Bushel basket	1
SWISS CHARD	Rhubarb	6 inch	3-4
	Fordhook Giant	6 inch	3-4
CHERRY TOMATO	Tiny Tim	6 inch	2-3
	Pixie Hybrid	6 inch	1
	Small Fry	6 inch	1
	Patio Hybrid	8 inch	1
	Sweet 100	Bushel basket	1
PLUM TOMATO	Veeroma	Bushel basket	1
	Roma VF	Bushel basket	1
WATERMELON	Sugar Bush	Bushel basket	1

This guide is just a sample of the many varieties that are well adapted to container growing. Seed catalogs often designate mini-, dwarf and compact varieties, many of which are good for container culture.

Adapted from: Cooperative Extension Service Ohio State University

CHAPTER 7

A WORLD OF YOUTH GARDENS

"Youths many times feel like the low man on the totem pole. Growing things not only gives them a sense of responsibility but shows they are needed. The plants *need them* for care. It keeps their minds busy. It's pleasing and fun. Gardening is a break from conventional learning. Something special for them to look forward to. It shows patience and caring, which is so needed in youth."

Christine Cotsman Wotowiec,
Garden Instructor
Garfield School
Medina, Ohio

HERE ARE THE PEOPLE AND ORGANIZATIONS BEHIND YOUTH GARDENS!

Gardens for young people come in many sizes and shapes, and they're found in many places...at schools, summer camps, nature centers and community gardens, to name just a few.

To give you a better idea about the kind of youth garden you might want to be a part of, we've outlined a wide range of garden projects and sponsors from around the country.

We hope these project descriptions give you the idea that, as far as youth gardening goes, where there are youngsters, there's a way to have gardens.

No one gardens alone

Sponsor: Summer Camp
Tamarack Farm
Plymouth, Vermont

Summer campers at Tamarack Farm depend on their garden—all 5 acres of it. Tamarack is one of six children's camps operated by the Farm and Wilderness Foundation. (For camp information, write to Executive Director, Farm and Wilderness Foundation, Plymouth, VT 05056.) The 5 acres of gardens have been providing much of the food for the camps for the past 45 years. In recent years, the 65 teenagers at Tamarack farm have built a 1,000-square-foot greenhouse from recycled materials to house the thousands of bedding plants needed to supply the gardens.

"Each summer," says past garden director Eve Pranis, "we set aside a special Food Day during which we eat only those foods that we've raised ourselves. These include the fruit and vegetable bounty, goods baked with our own grains, dairy products (butter, cheese, ice cream) and our own chickens. We have a veritable feast and learn not only how much we can provide, but also become aware of the dependency that we have on other sources for our sustenance.

No one gardens alone at Tamarack Farm. There's always a group to work with. And when the weeding occasionally becomes overwhelming, the whole camp is called in—65 people—and everybody joins in.

Tamarack farmers enjoy their harvest of salad greens and herbs.

FARM & WILDERNESS CAMP

Each group living at the camp provides for those who follow. The summer gardeners, in addition to providing plenty of fresh food for the main camping season, stock the freezers and root cellar for the fall and winter work crew programs.

"If you can give a helping hand, do it."

Sponsor: Individual
Mrs. Edna Boyle ("Mrs. Bee")
Charlestown, Massachusetts

Seven years ago Edna Boyle stopped a bottle fight between two groups of children at the Bunker Hill Housing development where she lives.

"I went in and got a broom to clean up the glass and one little girl said to me, 'I remember when this place really looked nice.'

I looked at her and said, "What do you say we try to do something about this!"

So Mrs. Boyle persuaded a group of youngsters to help her clean up debris and to plant flower and vegetable seeds around the development.

Her enthusiasm for cleaning and planting was catching—by the second planting season Mrs. Boyle (by then known as "Mrs. Bee" to her troops) had 150 kids, age four and up, growing food and flowers on about 5 acres of Housing Authority land.

Mrs. Bee has never had any formal training in agriculture or horticulture. Born and raised in Charlestown, she traveled much of her married life and has spent time in the Midwest. Her green thumb efforts are motivated by a philosophy she has carried through the years—"if you can give a helping hand, do it."

Leaders trained in gardening skills

Sponsor: Cooperative Extension Service
Extension Youth Garden Program
Milwaukee, Wisconsin

About 300 children are involved each year in Milwaukee's Youth Garden Program, sponsored and directed by the University of Wisconsin Extension Office.

The Extension budget supports the Milwaukee Urban Garden Program. They, in turn, get help from key volunteers around the city so the garden programs run smoothly. The question of leadership is a critical one. Says Barbara Pacey, staff horticulturalist in charge of educational efforts, "We look for and encourage any new groups which have strong adult leadership and a commitment to learning about gardening. We try to work with established youth groups, such as Boys and Girls Clubs and the Salvation Army, which already have strong leadership. This makes our work easier; we can train the leaders in basic gardening, and they, in turn, teach the children."

Group gardens are located on city and school land, at community centers, on private land, and also at a nursing home where youngsters garden with residents.

"We plowed the nursing home lawn and built some raised beds for the residents in wheelchairs," says past coordinator Maura O'Connor. "The interaction between the children and the senior adults was wonderful."

Noted O'Connor, "Some of our youth gardens are on city-owned lots in the central city. They are organized by neighborhoods or 4-H or block organizations. These gardens are more exposed to van-

dalism, but the neighborhood groups pull together and watch over them and the kids take tremendous pride in their plots."

In addition to its outdoor garden work, the Extension service offers educational programs in schools. They have developed a puppet show which is now available on videotape from the public library and the Extension office. It has become an excellent teaching tool that enables the organization to reach many children in the city.

Youth gardeners give seniors a helping hand in Milwaukee.

Over 500 students garden once a week

Sponsor: School (as part of regular curriculum)
Project Life Lab
Green Acres Elementary School
Santa Cruz, California

From a modest start with a 20-by 30-foot garden eight years ago, Project Life Lab has grown to include an acre garden, a large flower section, children's museum, fruit orchard, small 4-H livestock

barn, solar greenhouse and a student-made pond.

When teachers saw the success of their first small school garden, they sought and received a government grant to provide a garden-based science and nutrition curriculum. Now, all classes at the school (525 students) work at the garden site at least once a week. While one group is making cider, another group might be turning compost and yet another studying the oxygen cycle.

"The strength of the program," says Green Acres Life Lab Director Dawn Binder, "is that the garden becomes a living laboratory that incorporates as many subjects as possible." In addition to the standard Life Lab lessons, teachers are encouraged to use the garden setting for such areas as journal writing, theater and art.

Community involvement has also given the Green Acres faculty and students confidence that the Life Lab project will endure the ups and downs of educational funding. It was community effort which built the animal barn—merchants donated the wood, an architect provided his services for free and money was raised at a square dance.

A group of supporters—educators, farmers, business people and other community members—formed a non-profit organization (Friends of the Harvest) to boost Project Life Lab. Now called the Life Lab Science Program, the organization has been responsible for disseminating the "living laboratory" approach to elementary schools throughout California. Their three-volume curriculum, *The Growing Classroom* is an exemplary garden-based science and nutrition curriculum for second- through sixth-grade classrooms.

Project Life Lab

FRIENDS OF THE HARVEST

They bring their own plants home from school!

Sponsor: High School Vocational Education
Prairie du Chien Public Schools
Prairie du Chien, Wisconsin

Students in the Prairie du Chien high school "Hortication" courses have a lot to work with: a large greenhouse; a 93-tree apple orchard; a 40- by 40-foot bed of strawberries; a very large raspberry patch; a 40- by 80-foot vegetable garden; several colonies of bees; a school forest and a small nursery.

"Hortication" is the abbreviated term for horticulture education used by one of the administrators, Merle Frommelt. These hortication courses embrace gardening, berry culture, hive management, pomology, forestry, and greenhouse culture. Currently, the majority of students enrolled in the classes have had little or no experience with basic horticulture, whereas, several years ago, many of the students had a background in farming. After their hortication work, they know plenty about growing many varieties of fruits and vegetables.

The chief instructor in the program, Mark Pedretti, is employed under a 12-month contract because of the work necessary during the summer months as well as the school year. Students also volunteer their help with chores and share in the harvest during vacation months.

One prime feature of the program is that the students can reap benefits of the class by seeing and tasting the end results. Many students take home plants for their houses and backyard gardens. Over the years there have been upwards of 100 strawberry and raspberry beds started in back yards, farms and home gardens where there were none before.

Learning the raised bed method

Sponsor: Botanic Garden/ Arboretum
Hayes Regional Arboretum
Richmond, Indiana

After 20 years of the Arboretum's summer "Gardencraft" program for fifth to eighth grade youngsters, horticulture instructor Francis Parks recently led his 15 gardeners in building new raised bed gardens. It changed the look— and productivity—of the youth garden area.

Said Parks of the switch, "We had the best gardens ever. We mixed in plenty of peat moss and organic matter when we built up the beds."

The Gardencraft program, one of about 20 Arboretum summer offerings for youngsters, starts in May and concludes in October with a gala harvest party for gardeners and their parents in the Nature Center Auditorium.

The gardeners meet on Saturdays until the school year winds up, and then on Tuesdays and Fridays through the summer.

Gardeners pay $10 and the Arboretum furnishes the seeds, plants, tools and instruction for each youngster to tend his or her own 8-foot by 16-foot plot. In addition, there's a communal area where the group raises space-loving vegetables. Gardeners take home everything they grow in their own plots and share in the community produce.

Parks says the project is using only half the available garden land each year. "We let the other half lie fallow each year and alternate back and forth with the garden location."

To help parents enjoy the harvests hauled home by successful young gardeners, the Arboretum sponsored publication of the "Gardencrafter's Cookbook."

A garden experience for special youngsters

Sponsor: County Government and Non-Profit Group
Los Angeles County and Descanso Garden Guild, Inc.
La Canada, California

Descanso Garden Guild, a nonprofit group, is known throughout Southern California for supporting the county-owned Descanso Gardens in La Canada. One of the Guild's most important projects is its gardening class for special education children in the city and county schools.

The program began in 1960 with students from one school for

126

the handicapped and has since expanded to schools in numerous cities. Program Director Connie McKenney said there are about 15 classes per year, with about 12 students per class. Some of the students are mentally and physically handicapped; some are trainable mentally retarded; some are blind and some have academic learning problems. Each student works in the garden 90 minutes each week.

The school and gardening calendars mesh well in the Los Angeles area. In the fall of the year, students plant vegetables such as radishes, turnips, lettuce and broccoli for a winter and spring harvest. Cyclone fences are lined with rows of colorful bulbs, annual flowers, wildflowers and berries. In the spring, they plant corn, beans, squash, onions and other warm weather vegetables. Now that they have installed an automatic irrigation system, some children garden through the summer and the schools have raised their own Halloween pumpkins for the first time.

Children take their produce back to their schools and homes with a great sense of pride and

accomplishment, says past director Betty MacInnes. "We had an autistic boy once who was about to be sent to a special institution because there was just no way anyone could reach him. On harvest day he brought all his vegetables to the principal's office to show them off and he spoke his first words."

'Big Brothers' volunteer to help
Sponsor: Garden Club
Men's Garden Club
Stow, Ohio

"We have 300 gardens for youths along with our 200 plots for senior and adult citizens," says Men's Garden Club member Carl Horst, one of club's big boosters of youth gardening.

The youth gardens, supported also by the Stow Parks and Recreation Department, are free for youngsters. Horst says the program is designed "to attract and provide an opportunity for conscientious youths to learn gardening by growing vegetables and flowers."

Youths must register for garden plots before mid-May. Then the club has a "preview" program featuring slides of planting, weeding and harvesting techniques, plus some refreshments for youngsters and their parents.

After plots are assigned—all at one location—youngsters get a "Big Brother" from the ranks of club members. Horst says the Big Brothers are expected to work 20 or 30 hours with youngsters over the season. "We want to coach them in planning and caring for the garden. Maybe some will win ribbons for clean, weedless gardens featuring a good variety of vegetables and some beautiful flowers."

A farmers market for teen growers
Sponsor: Extension Service Endicott, N.Y.

About 25 teenagers in Tioga County, New York, are "growing for the market" in a 4-H sponsored project which has the theme "Earn and Learn."

The youths, some of whom earn $3,000 during the summer, get planning and technical help from Extension agent Frank Wiles, who helped launch the program 10 years ago.

The youngsters garden at home and usually get relatives or older friends to truck their produce to the Endicott (pop. 16,000) Farmer's Market which operates every Thursday and Sunday.

Said Wiles, "The best-selling crops are snap beans and pickling cukes. That's because most commercial growers don't want to do all that hand harvesting."

The market welcomes other growers, but older 4-H youths are in charge of the operation and draw managers' salaries.

The keys to a successful farmer's market, said Wiles, are continuing support from the merchants in the area, cooperation from police, enough parking, and plenty of potential shoppers in the area.

Wiles said one teenage brother-sister team earned almost $4,000 in 1982, "even though it was not a great growing year in this area."

Wiles recruits new gardeners every year by holding special meetings, speaking at schools and other youth group meetings. The job is getting harder and harder each year. "I'm concerned about it," said Wiles. "Kids 13 or 14 years old are the best age for this program, but for most of them the idea of 4-H, and of turning the soil is not that exciting," he said.

"Their peers tend to turn them off. But when one gets turned on to growing and earning some money, it's a different story."

Said Wiles, "The kids learn about life, about work, and about being with people. The first time they take their vegetables to market, it's frightening for them. But after a few weeks, it's in their blood."

Planting trees, "so that tomorrow will be beautiful"

**Sponsor: Cherry Creek Schools Cunningham Elementary Year-Round School
Denver, Colorado**

There's a terrific food gardening program at the Cunningham Elementary School, but a program of planting trees on the school land for the past 21 years has been just as important.

During the past several years, classes of third and fourth graders met twice each week. Past instructor Virginia Foster worked with the garden group, while Billy Foster guided pupils on tree or trail work and in flower planting.

A virtual school arboretum has been planted by Cunningham pupils over the years. Dozens of trees that are now flourishing were planted by past students. Species include Siberian Elm, Ponderosa Pine, Honey Locust, Yellow Dogwood, Russian Olive and others. After 21 years of tree planting, the campus landscape plan is complete and the Fosters, now retired, continue working in the gardening program.

Says Billy, "Our approach to gardening and tree planting has been primarily organic. We have

emphasized the history of human effort in growing food and fiber. In all our science activities we have managed to live with nature—the magpies, cottontail rabbits, robins, orioles, meadowlarks, bull snakes, and garter snakes."

Speaking of the importance of the tree plantings, Billy quotes the Arbor Day Foundation, "Like children, trees offer promise for the future. They are a way of insuring that tomorrow will be beautiful, that life will go on."

A "franchise" school garden

Sponsor: Mountain School Vershire, Vermont

No one has ever counted the total number of institutional buildings in the U.S. that house and feed students. But if they all used resident help to grow and harvest their own food, the savings could run into millions of dollars.

Eliot Coleman, a master gardener, has worked out a way to help such a thing happen. He got his idea from, of all places, the McDonald's fast-food chain.

Coleman points out that once McDonald's found the right formula,

it then examined every aspect and reduced it to a step-by-step operation that could be taught and reproduced precisely anywhere. Franchises followed the lesson plan, and the success of the fast-food chain is legendary.

Coleman has devised what he calls "a new McDonald's farm." It's a system by which institutions can plan food gardens, work out appropriate techniques and amounts of space, use efficient but not over-expensive tools, even how to handle seasonal labor demands at schools which don't have residents in summer.

The new McDonald's farm is "a food production system in which 5 acres, properly managed, will provide all the fresh and frozen produce needed to feed 200 people. And," he adds emphatically, "it will save money." It took him 15 years to develop the gardening format and because of the way he teaches it to others so they can duplicate it, he calls it a "franchise."

He believes his franchise idea is efficient, productive and simple enough that other institutions will give it a try. He points out that in most of the country, spring and fall are the labor intensive times for growing a large-scale garden. Even in schools where students are not present in summer, they are on hand at these crucial times.

The Coleman system requires a total capital investment of under $5,000 for tools. For optimum efficiency, he calls for a large tiller (14 horsepower); a professional, precision one-row push seeder; two manually-operated wheel hoes; and assorted smaller special hand tools.

"You don't have to hunt for a market for what you grow," Coleman tells school garden enthusiasts, "and your labor costs are almost free." The producers are also the consumers, while commercial growers have to pay all employees and then hunt for a market to sell their produce.

Unfortunately, there's no textbook or film yet detailing Coleman's ideas. But Eliot is getting the word out through summer seminars and tours. For information about the Coleman system, you should write directly to Eliot Coleman, c/o Mountain School, Vershire Center, VT 05079.

Eliot Coleman

Growing a world of love

Sponsor: Universal Children's Gardens
New York City, N.Y.

For several years now, Sandy Hinden along with supporters of "Universal Children's Gardens," has been seeking to help establish a thousand children's gardens around the world. Hinden's group envisions at least one children's garden in

every capital city "as a symbol of international peace and prosperity, achieved through harmony with nature."

Says Hinden, coordinator of UCG, "Life is a precious gift for us to experience and then to pass on to the next generation. While we are alive, we are given the chance to affect the quality of life as it exists during the age we live in. If we are conscious, we recognize what is important and not important, and what we *can* do to help develop life on our planet.

"During our age, the big challenge is to convert weapons into food, slow down our population growth, clean our environment, and create work for people to produce meaningful products.

"To help solve some of these problems," says Hinden, "we are creating Universal Children's Gardens to teach children in all nations to grow food and preserve the environment. The children learn to work and play together, they learn that children all around the world can be their friends and that each culture is like a different beautiful flower."

In 1981 New York's Queens Botanical Gardens sponsored a pilot Universal Children's Garden, with 55 children from 33 nations. "They began discovering the full potential of children's gardens to grow food, flowers, trees, and friendship," said Hinden.

Adds Hinden, "We are really serious about growing a Planet of Love. It *is* possible. All the resources and tools are available. Sometimes miracles just take a long time to unfold. Growing a Planet of Love takes patience, understanding, caring, and providing the proper amount of nourishment, weeding and healing of dis-ease...like any good garden."

For more information on Universal Children's Gardens, contact Sandy Hinden, UCG, 19 Post Street, Glen Head, New York 11545.

The Albert Schweitzer Universal Children's Garden in Great Barrington, Massachusetts.

School garden transforms city block

Sponsor: School
P.S. 173
New York, New York

In a city neighborhood in northern Manhattan, largely devoid of greenery and gardens, eight elementary classrooms, organized by teacher Paula Bower, have transformed a city-block-long strip into a thriving, educational garden.

The classrooms use the garden not only for science lessons, but for many other curriculum areas including history, math, art and music. One section has been set aside for growing a native American garden to integrate into social studies lessons. The students decided to start a garden newspaper with the hope that each class will contribute articles relating to their gardening experience.

Perhaps the greatest reward of this gardening experience has been the pride that the children have developed as a result of improving the beauty of their neighborhood. People in the neighborhood have responded by loving and protecting the garden from vandals. "The garden," says Bower, "is a great source of pleasure to the neighbors. The many senior citizens in the area walk back and forth to look at it. This year we finally met the man who had been sneaking rose bushes into the garden."

The children have established a special rapport with members of a local senior center. The seniors plant seeds and raise transplants in the spring that the children can plant outdoors in the garden. Bonds have developed beyond the bounds of the garden and seniors and children have found many other activities to share.

Bower's dream is that the P.S. 173 gardening program will serve as a model for the entire school district to raise awareness and interest regarding the value of school gardening and to ultimately reach the district's 20,000 children.

Horticultural therapy raises self-esteem

Sponsor: Therapeutic Center
Crittenton Center
Kansas City, Missouri

Horticulture Therapy is a program that is well respected by the staff at the Crittenton Center, a residential and day treatment program for emotionally disturbed children. The primary benefits of gardening, says horticulture therapist Scott Dexter, are that "it gives the children a sense of belonging.

They plant seeds and are involved in a life process that they can appreciate, be responsible for and share with others. The experience raises their self-esteem and helps build relationships with other peers and adults working with them."

Aspects of the program include a plant hospital where children learn to care for sick plants, a plant sale business in which clients start plants from seeds and cuttings to be sold to other residents and staff, an environment/nature awareness program, landscaping, an indoor plant care business and a 1½-acre vegetable garden.

The horticultural therapy programs have been strengthened in recent years by coordinating with the Men's Garden Club's 'Gardening from the Heart' program. Garden Club members meet with clients once a week for a short explanatory session followed by a hands-on participation of children in the gardens, greenhouse or nature study room. The projects generally require follow-up care by the children. For instance, one garden club member started about 200 cuttings with the children which were later repotted and used in a spring plant sale.

Regarding the role of horticulture in therapy, Dexter says "There is a non-threatening aspect to nature. A plant is non-discriminatory and it will respond. If not taken care of, it will wilt...This is a human lesson the children feel; we don't have to tell it to them."

YOUTH GARDEN PORTRAITS

The following "portraits" of youth garden projects around the country were written by project leaders themselves. The joys and occasional frustrations of leading a youth garden effort are revealed in these brief articles.

Extra hours of work make gardening a success

By Bob Peak
Teacher
School Gardening Project
Plaza Park School
Evansville, Indiana

A number of years ago, my fifth and sixth grade science students (approximately 160 children) started various kinds of plants in milk cartons on a sunny shelf in my classroom. They watered them, monitored their growth, studied their similarities and differences and then transplanted them at their homes.

After a couple of years, I decided it might be a good experience for my sixth grade students to grow some of the vegetable transplants in a demonstration garden in the courtyard of our school. We had about 720 students in kindergarten through eighth grade. The school is now a middle school with 550 students in grades six through eight.

In our first year, we planted sweet corn, tomatoes, peppers, zucchini squash, cucumbers, and pumpkins. All of the plants except the corn were started from seeds in the classroom and transplanted in the garden. Fortunately my classroom has a southern exposure which creates a greenhouse effect and lends itself very nicely to starting and maintaining seedlings.

We had moderate production from our plants, and we were particularly successful with tomatoes and peppers. Some of my students had never seen some of the crops we grew except in a grocery store.

All of our fruits and vegetables are now given to two local charitable organizations, a church-sponsored food pantry for elderly or disadvantaged inner city residents and the battered womens' shelter in Evansville. We hope this aspect of our gardening program will help our students develop an awareness of some of our social problems and ways that one can help others.

In order to include my fifth grade science students, we expanded our garden to a site that is 25 feet by 50 feet and we grew tomatoes, green peppers, potatoes, sweet corn, cucumbers, zucchini, snap peas, watermelons, broccoli, carrots, and radishes.

Up to now, space in my classroom for growing transplants has been a limiting factor. Luckily, I've been able to convince our principal and faculty that a greenhouse is a sound investment in the future of our students and the school. Several teachers on our staff are constructing the 10-foot by 20-foot aluminum and glass greenhouse in the courtyard, and we intend to sell vegetable seedlings from it next spring. Our profits will be used to purchase more greenhouse equipment or to further enhance our gardening program.

Obviously, one must make quite a commitment to a gardening program and must work many extra hours to make it successful. However, as an outdoor learning experience, I think it's unparalleled and should be an integral part of nearly every elementary science curriculum. Perhaps one of my sixth graders, Angie Jordan, summed it up best one day while digging in the garden when she said, "I didn't know that work at school could be so much fun!"

BOB PEAK

Week by week in an "A-OK" garden

by Christine Cotsman Wotowiec
Summer Gardening Program
Medina Joint Vocational Schools
Medina, Ohio

Our program lasted only 5 weeks last season—June 14 through July 14—but we accomplished a tremendous amount in this time.

Thirty-eight children participated in the gardening program, most with learning disabilities, some physically and mentally handicapped.

On gardening days, I met the young gardeners at Sidney Fenn Elementary School and with their teachers and aides, we caravaned to the Medina Vocational School.

There, each child had a 3-foot by 3-foot area of his own to plant and tend. We had two extra for demonstrations.

The first week, we planted radishes, lettuce and onion sets. Each child was given a name marker for his staked plot. Seeds and tools were distributed. This was the hard part because we had only one tool for each four children.

Pete Wotowiec, coordinator of the horticulture programs at the Vocational School, helped me guide the children.

The soil the first week was very moist but we still got everything planted. Some children received help with their plantings.

During the second week, we observed the plants which were germinating. To give the children a worms-eye view of what a sprouting seed looks like, I pre-sprouted some bean seeds so they could look at them. They also planted some nasturtiums and learned about companion planting.

After planting we took a tour of the Vocational School's greenhouse. There the kids learned how plants grow under glass and saw the many different varieties of plants grown there. A big favorite was a "Sensitive Plant" which temporarily wilts when touched. The automatic sprinkling system was their favorite tool in the greenhouse!

The children had a chance to do some planting in the greenhouse. This way they got to plant and learn about seeds, whole plants, and also cuttings.

The third week was my favorite week, in part because people from the Medina Sun Sentinel (our local paper) showed up. I demonstrated cultivating and thinning and compared it to combing your hair: 1. it's for looks; 2. it's to get unwanted things out (in hair, lint etc., and in soil, stones); and 3. it improves health. I also explained that you wouldn't comb your face because it would hurt, so you don't cultivate on the plants. The results were fantastic! They worked so hard with their tools and were so patient waiting for their turn.

All work and no play makes a program boring, so after hard work we built scarecrows. I had enough materials and hay ready for two scarecrows. It went over great. They all got a chance to stuff and build, and when completed, we placed a scarecrow at each end of the garden.

Our fourth week was devoted to maintenance. Most children enjoyed re-cultivating and learning about beneficial and harmful insects. We talked about storage and preserving of harvest and surplus and I showed them dried corn on the cob. They each received their own cob and got to "de-seed" it. We added sunflower seeds to it and they each had a bag full of wildlife feed to take home.

The fifth week was simple. We went back to the Vocational School's pond and learned about water plant life. The youngsters all got treated to watermelon and then we went on a hike before we returned to the garden plot.

Even though we were together only five weeks this year, these kids learned and experienced more about gardening and plant life than some do in a full summer.

Some aides mentioned the youngsters who were doing very well in the garden program were the ones that were the most "troublesome" in their classes.

The more handicapped, emotionally disturbed, and troublesome the child, the more he or she responded. We learned this from watching expressions, smiles or frowns, and hearing comments. The ultimate success for me was when one of the children hugged me and said, "I love you." The teenagers can be evaluated if they talk to you, or follow you, or most importantly, touch you. At that age, a soft punch on the arm followed by a smile could mean that everything is "A-OK."

The children asked for a sign, "No Adults Allowed!"

**By Louise Bastable
Garden Coordinator
North Shore Junior Gardeners
Middleton, Massachusetts**

We'd had our gardens for seven years, and when one of our three sites was enlarged from 34 gardens to 90, we decided to have more gardens for children. Before long we had 30 children signed up for the group which Barbara Dennis and I were going to teach. There were also 20 Grange children and a group of Laotian children gardening on our land. That was quite a few children with no tools other than our own.

When Barbara and I started our classes, the gardens had all been marked out with each child's name on their garden. Each plot was 6 feet by 10 feet. We were startled when not even half of the children that signed up came to first class. But the ones who did were very excited.

We soon realized how lucky we were that not everyone showed up. I had been teaching adult gardening classes and thought the children would present no problem. It was all going to be very easy. I had all the seeds filed in a big box so they would be easy to pass out. But while we were explaining the proper use of the tools, one little boy dumped the whole box of seeds into the dirt. I had asked that no one touch the box, but he just wanted to see what we were going to plant.

While we were showing them how to prepare the ground before planting seeds, the boy with the box of seeds was digging a pit and so was the girl down the other end. We (teachers??) smoothed out their gardens and went on with how to

plant the seeds, but our two diggers were back at it again. We were going to plant sunflowers along the back fence of each of the gardens. While I was searching through the jumble of seeds to find a package for each child, Barbara was still filling in holes made by the diggers. By this time I had had it. I told them, "One more hole and I'll bury you in it!"

That put a stop to the fun and games for a time, but I had an inkling I was going to learn plenty about working with children.

We later discovered that some of the mothers signed up their children for gardens either to have an extra garden for themselves, or for us to baby-sit while they gardened. We made the rule that we were available during class only, unless special arrangements were made. Also, no adults were to be allowed in the children's gardens. The children loved this and asked for a big sign saying, "No Adults Allowed."

Our garden classes got smaller but the children who came were very eager to learn. They did a much better job than the adults I taught at the community gardens. They didn't like to weed any better than the adults did, though. One little girl

asked, "Are we going to do good stuff next class or are we going to have to weed?"

Our children were ages six to nine. They learned to plant just about everything. Each had three tomato plants. They planted onion sets, beans, radishes, carrots, summer squashes and bush cucumbers. It seemed every week the seeds they planted the previous week were up and they were so excited about that.

The children learned things we were not even aware of. One day, I found a tomato hornworm in one of the adult's gardens. I picked it off with part of the branch and put it into a plastic bag to show the children. The next class a six-year-old girl told me she had a hornworm on her tomato plant. I asked where it was. She told me she didn't know but she showed me its droppings. She had noticed them in the plastic bag. I had never mentioned them.

Next year these children will be in an advanced class with a larger garden. They will also plant potatoes because they had so much fun helping to dig them in their parents' gardens. It was like a treasure hunt. They would gladly help dig potatoes.

Louise Bastable

Home gardener spreads joy and know-how

by Carol J. Coffey
Coordinator
Future Gardens of Glenn County
Orland, California

Why do plants need rain? How come peas grow in pods? What do ladybugs eat? Children's questions are endless. Only a garden can stir and satisfy curiosity in a way that can be seen, touched, and tasted.

While growing vegetables for several years in our northern California backyard, I experienced many rewarding lessons with my husband, Mark, and our two children, Tyrone and Jennifer. I wanted to expand horizons, reach out and share gardening adventures with others.

The first garden meeting we had was in early May, and 17 kids from 4-H, Camp Fire and Orland Schools, 6-16 years old, enrolled in my program. Later, people donated tomato seedlings so the youngsters would have a crop to tend until the garden was ready. We got plenty of help starting out from our farm advisor, Bob Sailsberry.

Kandace and Karen Burnett gave the youngsters a demonstration on how to put together a terrarium and our young members voted on a club name at the second meeting, "Future Gardeners of Glenn County." Some children grew gardens in my backyard, while others planted on their parent's land or at the community garden.

We had a project tour with parents providing transportation. Older participants were the photographers. Punch and snacks were served at the Burnett's home. Roberta Peterson was one gardener who proudly displayed her first yellow squash for us. "Now Mom has something to cook for dinner," she laughed. Too bad the snails ate her flowers.

We were all impressed with Sim Lely's large garden. He planted corn, tomatoes, marigolds, squash and pumpkins. He also knows the full name of the butterfly responsible for tomato hornworms (*Protoparc quinquemaculata*).

Cynthia Getter showed us her raised bed garden. She planted directly in rabbit manure from her family's rabbitry and crops really grew!

I tremendously enjoy working with the youngsters and seeing their excited expressions with each new discovery. The kids are watching, taking note of every little bug or weed. They grow right along with the plants. I believe that working a garden not only teaches a child useful skills, but also helps build self-esteem and promotes a caring attitude toward plants and people.

Some of my ideas for next year are to create team plots where up to six kids garden in a group. This will help younger gardeners gain experience and confidence and will enable mothers to share transportation. We might also sell excess produce at the farmers market to raise money.

I'll also start earlier and teach garden design, planning, record keeping, insects, trees, flowers, solar food drying, planting hay for animals. We'll have more field trips, too.

Carol Coffey and son, Tyrone

"Ask—you never know— you might get it!"

**by Carol Peralta
School Board Member and
Volunteer Garden Coordinator
Coupeville Elementary School
Gardening Project
Coupeville, Washington**

In these days of cutbacks, lay-offs, and financial uncertainty, schools have a hard time keeping up with the quality of education we all demand for our children. Many valuable programs have been severely reduced or eliminated in the name of economics. As educators wait in apprehension for the next axe to fall, it is refreshing to see a new project that is not only surviving but growing.

The Coupeville Elementary School Garden Project is in its infancy and owes its birth and growth to community support. Financially, the school could offer no support for the project, so other means were necessary to start offering gardening in the elementary school. The motto for our project became, "Ask—you never know, you might get it." The response has been overwhelming!

The Coupeville Lion's Club donated $250 for tools and fencing; we received $450 worth of tools and seeds through a Gardens for All grant. We were awarded a Title IV-C Grant of $830 for supplies and a curriculum. A local nursery and a seed company provided us with bedding plants and seeds.

We needed a place to store our supplies and the local Cemetery District allowed us the use of a storage shed.

Our water supply is less than adequate, but we've already had a pump donated for the well and the telephone company has dug a ditch to the power line so we can have the electricity to the well connected.

Many other volunteers have provided soil preparation, supervision and the emotional support that makes this type of project possible. But all of these things don't just come rolling in the door. The one thing I learned is that if I approach anyone with a positive request, whether they can help me or not, they will always return my interest. Never hesitate to make a request out of fear of the response.

Our goal was to teach math, science and reading through a garden project. Since we wanted to work through the school, the full support of the teachers was vital. If you can show teachers that you are not imposing an additional burden, and that the program will improve their effectiveness, they will be enthusiastic. We also had to get the support of the administration and the school board. Once the proper commitments are made, the rest is easy!

We were given the use of a 150-foot by 200-foot field near the high school gym but the rest was up to us. The soil was full of thick grass. I contacted a couple of farmers and asked them if they could plow it when they had their equipment out for their own fields. I also asked one if he would fertilize the site with some of the residue from his cows. The farmers went to work and the plot began to look like a garden site.

We are blessed hereabouts with a large rabbit population, so we needed a fence. Once more I delivered one of my "asks." I approached the Coupeville Lion's Club. I decided to shoot for the moon ($250) and also ask them to provide some of the tools we would need. We got the money and enough used chicken wire to enclose the garden. After the fence was up we made one more trip through the

garden with a rototiller. Then a group of volunteers staked and strung out the plots. The gardens were ready for the children.

The first year was a challenge, a learning experience and a success for the 60 students and for me. With good community support and financial help, it is possible to start out with little and end up with a new program.

During the summer the children and parents who continued in the garden found the experience to be invaluable. As the summer wore on, some of the children found the garden to be a little more than they bargained for. But we all learned from this and we'll plan next summer's garden as more of a community project.

A young Coupeville gardener.

Delinquent youths learn 'plants are like people'

by David G. Ardoff
Science Teacher
Boys Totem Town
St. Paul, Minnesota

"Hey teach! Whadda yah mean, I planted the seeds too deep? It says right here on the back of the seed package to spade the ground one foot deep!"

"You're right, Jim. But if you look a litte further, it says how to sow the seeds. Doesn't it say that to plant cucumbers we should first spade the soil 1 foot deep and make a group of five seeds placed in a ring about 2 inches across; and then to cover the seeds with ½ inch of fine soil?"

"Oh shucks! I thought it said I should plant the seeds 1 foot deep! Will they still grow?"

Learning to follow directions is only one of many learning experiences gardening provides for delinquent youth at Boys Totem Town, a residential treatment center for delinquent youth located in St. Paul, Minnesota.

Our garden was both fun and educational. Our classes found that you could make a square corner if you measure a distance along each side of the fence, find the square root of the sum of the squares of these numbers and use the resultant measure to move the legs of the fence to the correct distance, thus making a 90 degree angle. The same procedure was used in making square corners for the compost bin which was 8 by 16 feet in size.

Our youths not only gained a sense of appreciation for plants, but quickly found that plants have needs that are not much different than their own. They found plants need a good home and proper food, water and protection; and, they need lots of love and care if they are to grow and flourish.

Most important, the garden work gave residents time to think, to feel, and to expose their concerns about their roles in life.

Seventeen-year-olds who grew up in a blacktop-covered urban environment rushed to make their parents aware of their efforts and achievements. They couldn't wait to carry or send home the fruits of their labors.

Garden produce was common at many of our meals in the form of vegetables, salads and zucchini breads. Our residents found that some foods, previously approached with turned-up noses, were great when they had produced it themselves.

The residents also learned to share their bounty with others as well as with animals in the area. Some plants were left to provide a source of food to help animals get through harsh winter days.

Gardening, it seems, not only provides time to share feelings with each other, but for urban delinquent youth, it provides a productive leisure activity for the future. This is of special significance since the adage, "Idle hands are the devil's workshop," seems to be a contributing factor in the making of a delinquent youth.

A place to discover a new part of yourself

by John Smith
Teacher
Rancho Vejar
Santa Barbara, California

Rancho Vejar is a 3-acre urban farm located at the entrance to Santa Barbara's historic Mission Canyon. Rancho Vejar was incorporated as a private school in 1969, under the same charter that now runs a food bank, the local branch of the Hunger Coalition, a children's theater, and a small art museum.

The farm program until recently served about 10,000 school-aged children anually, half by way of field trip visitations to the farm itself and half by way of presentation at various local schools—such as our traditional Thanksgiving visits.

Field trip youngsters have watched the birth of pigs, tended sheep and goats, gathered eggs, tended beds of spinach and comfrey, curried the old grey mare, and used rabbit droppings to feed the many French-intensive vegetable beds. They've seen honey drawn from hives, forked compost bins, and sampled mustard-green soup cooked from farm raised greens and pork stock.

Rancho Vejar is a place where children of all ages have come to learn that growing food is an ancient human ritual involving plants and people and the natural cycles and rhythms of nature. But perhaps most important of all, Rancho Vejar has become a place where people can discover new or unexpressed parts of themselves, and gain a sense of community.

For troubled students, or those with a history of failure in school, the farm is a new vehicle for success.

The lessons in applied nutrition education and personal self-reliance are not based upon facility of language, and take place in the non-threatening outdoor environment. Teachers have commented over and over that a school farm or garden such as Rancho Vejar can effectively reinforce and complement the academic, social, perceptual and intra-personal goals of their class-rooms.

The most appropriate age group seems to be 7-12 years. Younger children tire mentally and physically in a shorter time, which complicates scheduling and transportation unless the site is on or very near the school grounds. Our own experience with secondary grade levels is limited, but we suspect that the "magic" of plant and animal life has less impact during the turmoil of adolescence. We'd like to be proven wrong.

I suppose the most valuable lesson I have learned from running the farm has been what a friend calls "the art of the possible." In 1970 I was fresh out of college, with degrees and credentials, enthusiasm, a head full of ideas... and no job, not even any enticing prospects. Schools in this area just didn't see any value or potential in the dream I had. So my only choice was to create a new school, and that was the beginning of Rancho Vejar.

Then the Farm Advisor advised me not to plant avocados, and so I planted avocados. Today, look at the trees sagging with fruit! Juvenile justice "experts" put their money into correction (instead of prevention), saying that there is no way to prove that prevention actually "prevents" crime. Well, we do know that correction increases crime; just look at the recidivism statistics. The Dairy Council continues its harangue about the Four Food Groups, with charts and dry lectures; with what results? More and more children arrive at school without breakfast, or after a breakfast of "porno food." Their food habits have become worse instead of better.

What am I saying in all of these examples? That here on a simple, low-budget farm we have been able to demonstrate the art of the possible, *disproving all these experts.* And it has been FUN! Students enjoy it, teachers respect it, parents appreciate it, and each and every one of us connected with Rancho Vejar over the years has gained a feeling of confidence, a personal blossoming, a sense of faith and community and commitment. And this experience has enabled all of us, I believe, to go forward with new dreams and desires—knowing that we will succeed, that our futures are laden with possibility.

We have always asked our students here at Rancho Vejar what they did *not* like about the place. As I look back through some of their journals I have saved over the years, I note that one student didn't like leaving at the end of the day, another said she didn't like being able to come here only one day each week. One didn't like the dust, another the mud (see, you can never hope to please everyone, anyway!). And, understandably, some do not like the fact that some of our animals are killed and eaten. I happen to cringe a bit when some of our plants are killed and eaten. That's farm reality. I won't pretend that living and dying are not interconnected, any more than I will deny children their rights to free speech and orderly protest.

This farm, any farm, is a place for growth and introspection and examination of the real world. It is a living opportunity to realize and apply the harmony and magic of nature. It is a superb opportunity for students to discover and rediscover themselves in their web of society and nature. It is a challenge for teachers to re-examine their teaching style, to question and expand the curriculum. It is a place and time for all of us to join together in creating our own future.

A Rancho Vejar harvest.

RAY BORGES

Editor's note: Although the Rancho Vejar program is currently in "crop rotation," as administrator John Smith relates, there are plans to start it up again in the future.

137

Gardening to end hunger
by Joseph Kiefer
Hunger Education
School Garden Program
Montpelier, Vermont

The Central Vermont Community Task Force Against Hunger, a coalition of state and community groups, was formed in 1983 to investigate the growing problem of hunger in our community. I became the education coordinator and hit upon the idea of involving students in public schools to address this local problem. I knew that our children were in need of creative challenges. Then it suddenly came together. Why not involve the students in a school gardening program that emphasizes growing food for the local emergency food shelves?

Since that day, hunger education to dispel the myths of the world hunger and to address the hunger that exists in our own communities has been adopted into several local school curricula.

The Hunger Education/School Garden Program, a project of the Institute for Social Ecology, has been gaining momentum and interest from all parts of Vermont and around the country. What really separates this program from other school garden programs is the connection to the issues of world and local hunger. This is the context for our science-based garden program. I now act as a school garden consultant, working with teachers to plan garden-based curriculum and to develop permanent garden science labs.

Students in this program engage in activities and role playing regarding food distribution as it relates to world hunger. As a result they gain insight into the inequities of food distribution and become

aware of the abundance that exists but is poorly distributed. The feedback from this program has also been encouraging. Parents are delighted that now their children can't wait to come to school.

In addition to growing food plants around and in the school, we're teaching the students how to teach others about food growing. This part of the program has become contagious; it's an opportunity for children to actively address a world and local problem and to feel that they can be part of the solution.

The real excitement of the Hunger Education/School Garden Program is that many spin-offs have been initiated by the students and community. In the 1985-1986 school year our Lettuce Eat Garden Group (an intergenerational school/community garden club) maintained a monthly emergency food drive; built community support by seeking donations of garden supplies; became regular venders at the Montpelier Farmers' Market; donated food to local senior citizen centers; supported our local family farmers by writing letters of support; donated fresh

produce from our permanent school garden to our local emergency food shelf and maintained both our flower and vegetable gardens.

The harvests reaped by this program have far exceeded our initial expectations. Empowering students is what education should be about, and we are proving that it works. Our next project is a sixth grade press conference during which the students will outline their plans for addressing 'Hunger and the Farm Crisis in Central Vermont.' They will announce a statewide sixth grade poster competition on 'A Vermont Without Hunger' and 'Saving the Family Farms in Vermont.'

Through the Hunger Education/School Garden Program we have learned that students respond enthusiastically to experiential education that has relevance and meaning. Schools can take on a new role as institutions that are concerned with the present and future health of the community.

Joseph Kiefer and his gardeners.

139

Note: To facilitate your locating these resources, we have included publishers' addresses and prices for books that are still in print and available through the publisher. Try your local library and bookstores for out of print books.

YOUTH GARDENING

A Basic Curriculum Guide For School Gardens. Diane L. Peterson. University of California Cooperative Extension, Contra Costa County, 1700 Oak Park Blvd., Pleasant Hill, CA 94523. $4.40. Provides general information on establishing a school garden site and offers ideas for integrating it into a K-8 curriculum.

Breaking Ground: A Guide for School and Youth Gardening Programs. Debbie Eglit Tidd, 1986. The San Francisco League of Urban Gardeners, 515 Cortland Avenue, San Francisco, CA 94110. $25. A clearly written, informative guide containing program and curriculum development ideas for educators, parents, volunteers and program leaders interested in starting youth gardening programs. Contains an extensive annotated bibliography.

Bringing Home The Bacon: School Gardens & Home Careers in Urban Farming. John Smith, 1980. Rancho Vejar, Inc., 37 Mountain Dr., Santa Barbara, CA 93103. $3, postpaid. A case study of Rancho Vejar youth garden and farm program and ideas for integrating gardening with classroom studies. Inspirational and informative.

A Child's Garden. Chevron Chemical Corp., revised 1984. Chevron Chemical Public Relations, 200 Bush St., San Francisco, CA 94120. $.50; free to teachers. Outdoor activities, experiments and explorations for elementary school gardeners.

Children's Gardens: A Field Guide for Teachers, Parents and Volunteers. Bremner and Pusey, 1982. Common Ground Program, 2615 South Grand Ave., Room 400, Los Angeles, CA 90007. $8.14. A great resource packed with how-to and plenty of educational activities for young gardeners.

Exploring the World of Plants and Soils. National 4-H Council, 7100 Connecticut Avenue, Chevy Chase, MD 20815. A lesson and activity series of 5 booklets that cover the basics of soils, plant characteristics, plant reproduction, etc. Available at minimal cost. Contact your local 4-H office or write to Educational Aids at the above address.

The Growing Classroom. Project Life Lab, 3rd printing, 1985. Life Lab Science Program, Santa Cruz County Office of Education, 809 Bay Avenue, Capitola, CA 95010. $40 for 3 volumes (includes postage). An exciting 3-book curriculum for establishing a garden-based science and nutrition program for grades 2-6.

Ladybugs and Lettuce Leaves. Project Outside/Inside, 1982. Center for Science in the Public Interest, 1755 S Street N.W., Washington, DC 20009. $6.95, student's book. $8, teacher's book. A solid gardening and environmental education curriculum for youngsters in grades 4-6.

Project Roots. Lansing School District, 1981. 2130 W. Holmes Rd., Lansing, Michigan 48910. $110 for set of 3 books including instructor's manual, gardener's handbook, and student lesson book. The books form the groundwork of a science-based gardening curriculum for grades 3-9. They include information on organization, public relations, and gardening, plus slides to accompany gardening lessons.

Sembrar Y Crecer (To Sow and Grow). Meals for Millions/-Freedom From Hunger, 1986. P.O. Box 26525, Tucson, AZ 85726. An activity guide/curriculum for gardening and nutrition in grades K-3. Helpful ideas for integrating the theme of activities into other curriculum areas.

"Youth Employment Programs in Community Horticulture-A Resource Guide." Holly Kaufman and Larry Sommers, 1986. National Gardening Association, 180 Flynn Ave., Burlington, VT 05401. $3. This paper includes current information on financial and technical assistance, project ideas and keys to success for operating horticultural youth training and employment programs.

Audiovisual

"Gardens Grow Children"-Slideshow. National Gardening Association, 1986. 180 Flynn Ave., Burlington, VT 05401. Rental-$35/$20 deposit. An inspirational show that concentrates on the special considerations of gardening with kids. Covers proven methods and program approaches, school gardens, indoor programs.

"Get Ready, Get Set, Grow"–Video. Brooklyn Botanic Garden, 1000 Washington Avenue, Brooklyn, NY 11225. Package-$29.95. Introduces children to the wonder of plant growth and the basics of gardening. Available in VHS and Beta formats. Includes two booklets: *A Kid's Guide to Good Gardening* and *Ideas for Parents and Teachers.*

BOOKS FOR YOUNG GARDENERS

A Book of Vegetables. Harriet L. Sobol, 1984. Grades 1-4. Dodd Mead Publishers, P.O. Box 141000, Nashville, TN 37214. $10.95.

Being a Plant. Laurence Pringle, 1983. Grades 6-8. Thomas Y. Crowell Publishing Co., 10 E. 53rd St., New York, NY 10022. $11.70.

Corn is Maize: The Gift of Indians. Aliki, 1976. Grades K-3. Harper and Row Publications, Inc., Keystone Industrial Park, Scranton, PA 18512. $4.95.

Eat the Fruit, Plant the Seed. Millicent Selsan, 1980. Grades K-3. William Morrow and Co., Inc., 105 Madison Ave., New York, NY 10016. $11.75.

Eddie's Green Thumb. Carolyn Haywood, 1980. Grades 3-7. William Morrow and Co.

From Flower to Fruit. Anne Ophelia Dowden, 1984. Grades 5-6. Thomas Y. Crowell Publishing Co., 10 E. 53rd St., New York, NY 10022.

Gardening. Virginia Kirkus, 1976, Grades 4 up. Watts, Franklin, Inc.

Growing A Garden Indoors & Out. Katherine Cutler, 1973. Grades 4 up. William Morrow and Co.

How Seeds Travel. Cynthia Overbeck, 1982. Grades 3-6. Lerner Publishing Co., 241 First Ave., N. Minneapolis, MN 55401. $12.95.

In My Garden: A Child's Gardening Book. Helen and Kelly Oechsli, 1985. Grades 1-4. Macmillan Publishing Co., 866 3rd Ave., New York, NY. $12.95.

Indian Corn and Other Gifts. Sigmund Lavine, 1974. Grades 5-9. Dodd Mead Publishing Co.

Indoor Gardening. Fenton, 1974. Grades 4-10. Watts, Franklin Inc.

The Kids Garden Book. Petrich & Dalton, 1974. Grades 1-6. Nitty Gritty Productions.

Kids Outdoor Gardening. Paul Delulio, 1978. Grades 3-7. Doubleday and Co., Inc.

Mr. Plum's Paradise. Elisa Trimby, 1976. Grades K-3. William Morrow and Co.

My Garden, A Journal for Gardening Throughout the Year. Louise Murphy, 1980. Grades 1-6. Charles Scribner's Sons.

My Garden Companion: A Complete Guide for the Beginner. Jaime Jobb, 1977. Grades 4 up. Charles Scribner's Sons.

My Own Herb Garden. Allan Swenson, 1971. Grades 4 up. Rodale Press, Inc.

Play With Plants. Millicent Selsan, 1978. Grades 4-6. William Morrow & Co.

The Pumpkin People. David & Maggie Cavagnaro, 1979. Grades 1-4. Charles Scribner's Sons, 597 Fifth Ave., New York, NY 10017. $8.95.

The Reason for a Flower. Ruth Heller, 1983. Grades K-4. Grosset & Dunlap, New York, NY. $7.95

The Secret Garden. Frances H. Burnett, 1971. Grades 4 up. Dell Publishing Co., Inc., 1 Dag Hammarskjold Plaza, 245 E. 47th St., New York, NY $3.50.

Snips and Snails and Walnut Whales. Phyllis Fiarotta, 1975. Grades 2-6. Workman Publishing Co., 231 East 51st St., New York, NY 10022. $8.95.

Willie's Garden. Myra McGee, 1977. Grades 5 up. Rodale Press, Inc.

GARDENING INFORMATION

All About Fertilizers, Soils and Water. Cort Sinnes, 1979. Ortho Books. A detailed look at these important components of the vegetable garden.

The Bountiful Solar Greenhouse. Shane Smith, 1982. John Muir Publications, Inc., P.O. Box 613, Santa Fe, NM 87501. $8. Complete and easy to follow. Everything you need to know to grow food successfully in a solar greenhouse.

Directory of Seed and Nursery Catalogs. (updated yearly) The National Gardening Association, 180 Flynn Ave., Burlington, VT 05401. $3. Addresses and descriptions for over 200 companies, organized by type of catalog and product.

Down-to-Earth Vegetable Gardening Know-How. Dick Raymond, 1981. Garden Way Publishing/-Storey Communications Inc., Pownal, VT 05261. $7.95. Tips and information on planning, soil preparation, planting, weeding, disease and pest control, harvesting, soil building, compost and vegetable storage.

The Dried Flower Book. Annette Mierhof, 1981. E.P. Dutton, Elsevier-Dutton Publishing Co., Inc., 2 Park Ave., New York, NY 10016. $14.50. Information on raising, preserving and arranging dried flowers.

The Edible Indoor Garden. Peggy Hardigree, 1980. St. Martin's Press. Highly recommended for indoor gardeners. It offers a thorough explanation of basic plant needs, specific cultural requirements of many crops and an extensive resource list.

The Encyclopedia of Natural Insect and Disease Control. Roger B. Yepsen, Jr., 1984. Rodale Press, 33 E. Minor St., Emmaus, PA 18049. $24.95. The most up-to-date information regarding natural controls for pests and diseases in the garden and greenhouse.

The Encyclopedia of Organic Gardening. Staff of Organic Gardening magazine, 1978. Rodale Press, 33 E. Minor St., Emmaus, PA 18049. $24.95. A raft of how-to information on everything from beekeeping to vegetables.

Gardening. National Gardening Association, 1986. 180 Flynn Ave., Burlington, VT 05401. $19.95 (soft); $34.95 (hard). (non-members) The editors of *National Gardening* magazine have brought together all the latest gardening developments in this one big, informative volume to make it a comprehensive and up-to-date guide to growing fruits and vegetables.

How to Grow More Vegetables. John Jeavons, 1982. Ten Speed Press, P.O. Box 7123, Berkley, CA 94707. $8.95. The book clearly explains the high yield, biodynamic/French intensive method of gardening. Allows you to increase your harvest with less space.

Intensive Gardening Round the Year. Doscher, Fisher, Kolb, 1981. Stephen Greene Press. Practical know-how for intensive gardening techniques. A section is dedicated to special solar methods for lengthening the garden season.

Knotts Handbook for Vegetable Growers. Lorenz & Maynard, 2nd edition, 1980. John Wiley & Sons, Inc. 605 3rd Ave., New York, NY 10158. $24.50. Specific information and hard-to-find data (much in chart form) on such subjects as nutritional quality of plants, seed spacings, liming large fields, viability of seeds and much more.

National Gardening Association Gardening Series. Revised 1985. National Gardening Association, 180 Flynn Ave., Burlington, VT 05401. $15 (member)/$27.50 (non-member) for complete Garden Library of 11 books. Individual books, $2.50. Each book is a guide to growing, harvesting, preserving and cooking vegetables. Series includes: Lettuce & Greens; Potatoes; Beans; Onions; Cauliflower, Broccoli and Cabbage; Tomatoes; Peas and Peanuts; Cucumbers, Melons & Squash; Corn; Eggplant, Okra and Peppers; Root Crops.

The Organic Gardener's Complete Guide to Vegetables and Fruits. Editors of Rodale Press, 1982. Rodale Press, 33 Minor St., Emmaus, PA 18049. $21.95. An information-packed guide to growing, harvesting, and storing a wide variety of fruits and vegetables.

Rodale's Color Handbook of Garden Insects. Anna Carr, 1980. Rodale Press, 33 E. Minor St., Emmaus, PA 18049. $12.95. Includes over 300 color photographs of insects in egg, larval, pupal and adult stages. Life cycles, feeding habits, host plants, related predators and organic control techniques are covered.

The Self-Sufficient Gardener. John Seymour, 1978. Dolphin Books, Doubleday and Co. A comprehensive gardening book with lovely illustrations and thorough background information on most garden crops.

Square Foot Gardening. Mel Bartholomew, 1981. Rodale Press, 33 E. Minor St., Emmaus, PA 18049. $11.95. Easy-to-follow intensive gardening plans based on square foot plantings.

Your Nutritious Garden. National Gardening Association, 1984. 180 Flynn Ave., Burlington, VT 05401. $3.95. A 44-page beginner's guide to gardening, emphasizing growing vegetables for good nutrition.

FOOD AND NUTRITION

Choose Well, Be Well. California State Dept. of Education, 721 Capitol Mall, Sacramento, CA 95814-4785. A nutrition education curriculum series for grades K-high school. Includes curriculum guides and computer activities. (Guides-$8.00) Write for ordering brochure.

Community Food Education Handbook. Ellen Weiss, et al., 1980. MANNA, 4804 Charlotte Ave., Nashville, TN 37209. $6. A book for groups and individuals who want to start food education programs in their local schools, churches, co-ops and community centers.

Creative Food Experiences for Children. Goodwin and Pollen, Rev. 1986. Center for Science in the Public Interest, 1755 S. Street, N.W., Washington, DC 20009. $5.95 soft-cover. Written for adults working with pre-school and elementary age children, it includes activities, recipes, games and facts.

Eclipse of the Blue Moon Foods: A Guide to Teaching Food Education. Petit and Weiss, 1980. MANNA, Inc. 4804 Charlotte Ave., Nashville, TN 37209. $6. teacher guide, $2.50 student workbook, $1.50 family book. Activity oriented approach to exploring food preparation and processing, gardening and agriculture issues, food industry, energy in the food system and food and nutrition policies. For elementary age children.

Energy, Food, and You: An Interdisciplinary Curriculum Guide for Elementary Schools. Washington State Office of Public Instruction. First draft, 1977. Office of Environmental Education, 17011 Meridian N., Rm. 16, Seattle, WA 98133. $7 each. Two large books, a primary/intermediate and a secondary edition packed with activities on energy and food, farming, packaging, processing, advertising.

Food Scorecard. Wendy Wilson and Michael Jacobson, 1980. Center for Science in the Public Interest, 1755 S St., NW, Washington, DC 20009. Grades 3-6. $1. Covers nutrition basics by describing basic food groups and assigning scores based on nutritional value.

Food for the Health of It. Project Outside/Inside staff, 1979. Available through The Network, Inc., 290 S. Main St., Andover, MA 01810. High school nutrition curriculum that also examines the role of the food industry in shaping our diet.

Good for Me. Marilyn Burns, 1978. Yolla Bolly Press, Covelo, CA 95428. $7.95. Cartoon illustrations accompany material on nutrition, history of foods and the food industry. Written for youths up to junior high.

Nutra Lunches & Natural Foods. Sara Sloan, rev. 1979. Sara Sloan, P.O. Box 13825, Atlanta, GA 30324. $8.95. Menus, recipes, tips on organization and public relations, facts and figures from the award-winning NUTRA Food program in the Fulton County Schools. A brochure on other NUTRA publications available.

What's to Eat? And Other Questions Kids Ask About Food. USDA Year Book, 1979. Limited quantities available free through office of your member of Congress. Heavily illustrated book about food, nutrition; includes activities, recipes and games. For elementary age children.

World Hunger

Feed, Need, Greed. Food & Nutrition Group, 1980. Science for the People, 897 Main St., Cambridge, MA 02139. $5.50. A high school curriculum exploring food, resources and population.

Food First Curriculum. Laurie Rubin, 1984. Institute for Food and Development Policy, 1885 Mission Street, San Francisco, CA 94103. Grade 6. $12 plus postage/handling. A multicul-

tural curriculum about food and the roots of hunger and local action. 33 worksheet activities.

World Food Day Curriculum. The Food and Agricultural Organization of the U.N. National Committee for World Food Day, 1001 22nd St. NW, Washington, DC 20250. Grades K-12. A curriculum guide series designed with activities to help students consider world hunger issues.

OTHER RESOURCES

Environmental Education

Connections: A Curriculum in Appropriate Technology for Fifth and Sixth Graders. Joan Melcher, 1980. National Center for Appropriate Technology, P.O. Box 3838, Butte, MT 59702. $7.

The Edible City Resource Manual. Richard Britz et al., 1980. William Kaufman Inc., 1 First St., Los Altos, CA 94022. $14.95. This book, with a segment on youth gardening for elementary age students, explores urban agriculture pilot projects in Eugene, Oregon.

Growing Up Green. Hickaby & Skelsey, 1978. Workman Publishing Company, 231 East 51st Street, New York, NY 10022. $4.95. A project book and philosophy designed for adults and children gardening together.

Manure, Meadows and Milkshakes. Eric Jorgensen, Trout Black, Mary Hallesy, 1978. The Trust for Hidden Villa, 26870 Moody Rd., Los Altos Hills, CA 94022. $9.95. An environmental edu-

144

cation handbook with 88 activities to complement any youth garden program.

Naturewatch: Exploring Nature With Your Children. Adrienne Katz, 1986. Addison-Wesley Publishing Co., Jacob Way, Reading, MA 01867. $7.95. Includes 50 fun and easy-to-do projects for actively sharing the wonders of the natural world with your children.

Food Preservation

Guide to Food Drying. Phyllis Hobson, 1980. Garden Way Publishing.

Putting Food By. Ruth Hertzberg, Rev. 1981. Bantam Books.

Stocking Up. Carol Hupping, Rev. 1986. Rodale Press, Inc., 33 E. Minor St., Emmaus, PA 28049. $13.95. The latest edition of this thorough reference guide for preserving home-grown foods.

Greenhouses

The Bountiful Solar Greenhouse. Shane Smith. (see 'Gardening Books')

The Food and Heat Producing Solar Greenhouse. Yanda & Fisher, 1976. John Muir Publications, Santa Fe NM 87501. $8. One of the best basic primers on simple, low-cost solar greenhouses. Solar principles explained with construction details and horticultural information.

How to Build and Use Greenhouses. Jeff Williams, 1978. Ortho Books, Chevron Chemical Co., 575 Market St., San Francisco, CA 94105. $6.95. Large and small, build your own or packaged, with special sections on solar heating, hydroponics, coldframes and window greenhouses.

Garden Building Projects

Build it Better Yourself. Edited by William Hylton, 1977. Rodale Press, 33 E. Minor St., Emmaus, PA 18049. $24.95. Full construction plans for indoor gardening projects, making simple tools, coldframes, raised beds, birdhouses, food dryers, food storage bins, and lots more.

Wood Projects for the Garden. Edited by R.J. DeCristoforo, 1976. Ortho Books, Chevron Chemical Co., 575 Market St., San Francisco, CA 94105. $6.95. Plans for building containers, trellises, raised beds, benches, compost bins, worktables, etc. Basic carpentry skills and techniques explained.

Community Gardening

The Community Garden Book. Larry Sommers, 1984. National Gardening Association, 180 Flynn Ave., Burlington, VT 05401. $8.95. An informative guide for anyone who would like to turn vacant lots or unused land into productive community food gardens. Describes a broad range of program styles and sponsors and offers organizing tips, fund-raising ideas, and strategies for protecting land.

A Handbook of Community Gardening. Boston Urban Gardeners, edited by Susan Naimark, 1982. Charles Scribner's Sons, 597 5th Ave., New York, NY 10017. $7.95. An up-to-date text on organizing community gardens including historical background, site development, and helpful tips on managing food growing projects.

Weeds/Insects

Common Weeds of the United States. U.S. Department of Agriculture, 1971. Dover Publications, Inc., 180 Varick St., New York, NY 10014. $8.95.

Eat the Weeds. Ben C. Harris, 1969. Keats Publishing Inc., 36 Grove St., P.O. Box 876, New Canaan, CT 06840. $1.50

Exploring the Insect World. Margaret Anderson, 1974. McGraw-Hill Book Co., 1221 Avenue of the Americas, New York, NY 10020. $6.95

Golden Guide to Insects. Zim and Cottam, 1951. Golden Press, Dept. M, Western Publishing Co., Inc., 1220 Mound Ave., Racine, WI 53404. $2.95.

Group Games

The New Games Book. Andrew Fluegelman, editor. New Games Foundation, P.O. Box 7901, San Francisco, CA 94120. $7.95. Contains instructions for many creative, noncompetitive group games that involve people of all ages.

More New Games. Andrew Fluegelman, editor. New Games Foundation, P.O. Box 7901, San Francisco, CA 94120. $7.95

ORGANIZATIONS

American Community Gardening Association. (ACGA) c/o Chicago Botanic Garden, P.O. Box 400, Glencoe, IL 60022. The ACGA is a membership organization which acts as a network for disseminating information to support community gardening in the U.S. The group has a vast network of members across the country, many of whom are valuable resources for youth gardening information. They also publish a quarterly *Journal of Community Gardening.*

Center for Science in the Public Interest. 1755 S. Street, NW, Washington, DC, 20009. CSPI is a nonprofit organization which investigates and seeks solutions to problems related to science and technology. Publishes newsletter *Nutrition Action* and youth garden related books, posters and pamphlets.

Cooperative Extension Service. This is a government organization that provides gardeners with a wealth of information and advice on local gardening needs and problems. They also supply many helpful gardening publications free or at a reasonable price. To contact your local Extension Service Office, look under "Cooperative Extension" or under the name of your county in the phone book.

Institute for Food and Development Policy. 1885 Mission St., San Francisco, CA 94103. A research and educational organization that emphasizes a political perspective on food and hunger issues. Has a free publications catalog that lists books, curricula and other resources.

Men's Garden Clubs of America. (Gardening from the Heart Program). 5560 Merle Hay Rd., Johnston, IA 50131. This national organization has chapters in every state. The Gardening from the Heart Program encourages local clubs to reach out and establish partnerships with community groups in need of gardening assistance. Many successful partnerships have been formed with youth programs.

National Committee for World Food Day. 1001 22nd Street NW, Washington, DC 20437.

National Committee for World Food Day has developed a resource list of available written and audio-visual materials on teaching about world food and hunger.

The National Council for Therapy and Rehabilitation through Horticulture. 9041 Comprint Ct., Suite 103, Gaithersburg, MD 20877. NCTRH is a membership organization that promotes the use of horticulture and related activities in therapeutic and rehabilitative programs. Members have worked extensively with youth gardening programs.

National 4-H Council. 7100 Connecticut Avenue, Chevy Chase, MD 20815. This is the youth arm of the Cooperative Extension Service. The council offers programs, awards and educational aids to 4-H members, volunteer leaders and staff. They also publish a quarterly *4-H Leader* magazine. Your county Cooperative Extension Office can put you in touch with local 4-H programs.

National Gardening Association. 180 Flynn Ave. Burlington, VT 05401. A membership organization dedicated to helping people to be successful gardeners. NGA offers a youth gardening information packet, assistance in establishing youth gardening programs, educational materials for school gardening programs and numerous publications and slide shows. Publishers of *National Gardening* magazine.

National Junior Horticulture Association. 5885 104th St., Fremont, MI 49412. This organization promotes youth gardening by outlining projects, sponsoring contests and offering awards and incentives to indi-

viduals and youth groups involved in horticultural activities.

OXFAM America. 115 Broadway, Boston, MA 02116. An international agency that promotes self-help projects in developing countries. Has a free *Educational Resources Catalog* that lists books, curricula and other resources.

Universal Children's Gardens. P.O. Box 2698, Grand Central Station, New York, NY 10163. This group is helping to establish at least one children's garden in every capital city around the world as a symbol of international peace and prosperity.

Activity program:
    and children's motivation, 13-15
    for harvest party, 28
    planning, 18
    suggestions (list), 66-109
    see also Garden projects
Administrative support, 17
Animals:
    made out of vegetables, 103
    raising, 15
Asphalt lot, as garden site (with raised
    beds), 61
Awareness exercise, 94

Beans:
    dry, 65, 99
    interplanted with corn and squash, 88
    pole varieties, 68
    spacing, 66
Bird feeders, homemade, 100
Blackberry jam (how to make), 83
Block planting, 66
Blueprints from the garden, 86
Books of garden stories (list), 79
Broccoli:
    harvesting experiment, 67
    started indoors, 114
Budgets (samples), 5-7
Bug box, 97

Cabbage:
    interplanted with lettuce, 68
    spacing, 67
    started indoors, 114
    transplanting, 66
Calendars:
    for garden activities, regional, 22-24
    for indoor gardening, 25
Carrots:
    necklace made of, 103
    thinning (experiment), 69
Charades and skits, 92
Chard: harvesting experiment, 66
Coldframes: 46, 54
Communal garden area: 53
Community garden, as site for youth
    garden: 3, 18
Companion planting, 68
    see also Interplanting
Composting, 41-42, 54
    mini-project (in plastic baggies), 77
Concentration game, 95
Container gardening, 3, 117-119,
    table 120-121
Contests and competitions:
    concentration game, 95
    garden grants, 7
    pumpkin-sunflower (for size), 13
    riddles, 71
    see also Games
Contributions to garden project,
    tax deductible, 9

Corn:
    grinding and patty making, 102
    interplanted with beans and squash, 88
    rows vs. hills, 67
    started indoors, 114
Corn husk dull, 101
Cover cropping, 42
Cucumbers:
    indoor starting, 111, 114
    pickled in a bottle, 76

Dedication ceremony, 8
Demonstration garden, 53
Disabled children, as gardeners, 125
Dolls, corn husk, 101
Dryer for food, solar, 89

Edible landscaping, 3
Expenses:
    budgets (samples), 5-7
    minimizing, 4-5
Experimental garden projects, 66-69
Expert gardener, as consultant, 1-3, 19

Farmers market, 13, 126, 137
"Feely Box," 80
Fence, 43
Fertilizer and fertilizing, 37-40
    amount needed, *table* 38
    "manure tea," 90
    natural sources of, 38
    for seedlings, 114
    side-dressing, 38, *table* 40
Flour, made from wheat berries, 106
Flowers:
    drying, 104-105
    learning parts of, 78
Food dryer, solar, 89
Food sources, study of, 75
Fund-raising, 8-10
    at harvest time, 28

Games:
    catch the raccoon's tail, 87
    concentration, 95
    garden jeopardy, 72
    garden word scramble, 70
    riddles, 71
    skits and charades, 92
Garden programs, 123-137
    experiments, 66-69
"Garden Song," by David Mallett, 108
Germination of seeds:
    indoors, 112, 13
    temperature for, *table* 113
Grants, for garden programs, 7
Green manuring (cover cropping), 42
Greenhouse, solar, 54, 115
Grow Lab Program, 116
Growth charts for garden, 91

Handicapped children, as gardeners, 125, 129

Harvest party, 28
    sharing, 28
Home garden project, 3, 12
Hunger, activity, 73
    responding to locally, 28, 137

Indoor gardening, 111-116
Insect spray, homemade, 92
Insects: collecting, 97
Insurance, 20
Intensive gardening, 61
Interest in gardening, maintaining, 13-15
Intergenerational gardening, 2, 13, 129
Interplanting:
    cabbage and lettuce, 68
    corn, beans, and squash, 88
    see also Companion planting

Jam, blackberry (how to make), 83
Japanese beetle trap, 84
Jeopardy game, 72
Journal of garden, 70

Land (where to find it), 3, 18, 30
Landscaping, edible, 3
Layout of garden:
    design ideas, 53-54
    for (72) individual plots, 58-61, *illus.*,
    59-60
    sample plans, *illus.* 48-51, *illus.* 55-57
    Lead contamination of soil, 30-31
Leaders, 1-2
    individual experiences of, 130-37
    paid, 6, 12
    time required of, 13
    volunteer, 2, 12
Lettuce:
    interplanted with cabbage, 68
    starting indoors, 114
    in wide rows, 66
Lights, starting seedlings under, 112
    growing under, 115
Liming soil, 34

Mallett, David: "Garden Song," 108
Manure for garden, 37
"Manure tea," 90
Marking rows in garden, 81
Maze, plants grown in, 85
Melons:
    and black plastic mulch, 69
    indoor starting, 68, 114
Mint tea, solar, 87
Money requirements and resources,
    4-10
Motivation of young gardeners, maintaining,
    13-15
Mulch:
    for melons, 69
    for tomatoes, 68

Necklace made of carrots, 103
New Zealand spinach *vs.* spinach (experiment), 67

Onions:
    spacing of, 66
    started indoors, 114
Organizations (list), 144-145
Organizers, *see* Leaders

Parents, as garden experts, 2
Partnerships, with other organizations, 4
Paths in garden, 53
Peppers:
    fertilizing, 67
    started indoors, 114
"Pillow pak," 118
Planning garden project, 17-19
Planning garden site, *illus.* 48-51, *illus.* 55-57
    for (72) children, 58-61, *illus.* 59-60
    marking off plots, 58, 59
Plant press, homemade, 98
Plastic bag, plants grown in, 118
Plots, individual:
    for (72) children, 58-61, *illus.* 59-60
    marking off, 58, 59
Plowing garden, 36, 37
Praying mantis, raising, 74
Presses for plants, homemade, 98
Printing vegetable designs, 94
Public relations, 7-8
Publicity, 7-8
    and children's motivation, 13
    for recruiting participants, 17
Pumpkins:
    names inscribed on, 84
    started indoors, 114

Raccoon's tail game, 87
Rain gauge, homemade, 91
Raised beds, 61
Record-keeping for garden, 91
Recruiting participants, 17-18
Riddles, 71
Root-view box, 76
Roto-tilling garden, 36
Row markers, homemade, 81

Salad garden, 13
Salad of weeds, 96
"Sausage culture" (pillow pak), 118
Season extension, 46
Seasonal activities, by region, 22-24
Seedlings, starting indoors, *chart* 111, 112-15
Seeds:
    germinating indoors, 112-14, *table* 115
    saved and observed, 107
    sprouting experiment, 80
Sensory awareness exercise, 94
Side-dressing, 38, *table* 40
Signs in garden, 62

Singing, 108
Site for garden, 3, 18
    asphalt lot as, 61
    cleanup and improvement of, 33
    designs for (samples), *illus.* 48-51, *illus.* 55-57
    selection criteria, 30-33
Size of garden:
    and children's motivation, 13, 14
    and site selection, 32
Skits and charades, 92
Soil:
    compacting, experiment in, 69
    cost of improving, 4
    lead contamination of, 30-31
    liming, 34
    "soil-less," for seedlings, 112-13
    testing, 34
    topsoil, 34-35
    see also Composting; Fertilizer and fertilizing
Solar food dryer, 89
Solar greenhouse, 54, 115
Solar mint tea, 87
Soliciting donations, 8
Spinach *vs.* New Zealand spinach (experiment), 65
Spring garden, 13
    layout for, 55 and *illus.*
Squash:
    interplanted with corn and beans, 88
    started indoors, 114
    see also Zucchini
Story-telling, 79
Summer care of garden, 13
Surplus vegetables, donating, 8, 28
Swiss chard: harvesting experiment, 66

Tax deductions, for donations to garden project, 9
Tea, mint (solar), 87
Testing soil, 34
Theft from garden, 10-12
Tilling garden, 36
Time required for gardening, 13
Toad house, 82
Tomatoes:
    mulching, 68
    protectors for, 68
    pruning experiment, 67
    started indoors, 114
    transplanting, 69
Tools, 20
    care of, 90
    cost of, 4
    storage of, at garden site, 20
Topsoil, 34-35
Transplants:
    advantages and disadvantages of, 18-19
    starting indoors, *chart* 111, 112-14, *table* 115

Tree-planting project, 127
T-shirts, designs applied to, 81

Universal Children's Gardens, 128

Vacation from school, garden sustained during, 12-13
Vandalism, 10-12
Vegetable designs, printed, 94
Vertical gardening, 117
Volunteer leadership, 2, 12

Walkways in garden, 53
Water:
    availability of, 32-33
    bringing to garden, 43-45
    conservation tip, 45
    pipe system, installation of, 44-45
    plants' need for, 45
    for seedlings, 113
    storage of, at garden site, 44
Weeds:
    control of (experiment), 67
    edible, as salad, 96
Wheat berries, made into flour, 106
Wide rows of lettuce, 66
Word scramble game, 70
World hunger activity, 73
Worms, how to raise, 93

Zucchini: harvesting experiment, 68

ABOUT THE NATIONAL GARDENING ASSOCIATION

The National Gardening Association is a nonprofit member-supported organization established in 1972. NGA is dedicated to helping people garden successfully at home, in community groups, and in schools. We believe gardening adds joy and health to living while improving the environment and encouraging our appreciation for the proper stewardship of the earth.

The National Gardening Association is a clearinghouse of gardening information for 69 million gardening households in the United States. NGA's 200,000 members receive the color monthly magazine, *National Gardening*. Members can also use the NGA Gardening Answering Service, receive discounts on NGA's many books and videos, and swap seeds, tips, and recipes with other members.

A major focus of our education programs is to promote gardening with children. Gardening is a hands-on method of exciting children about science, nutrition, and the environment. In thousands of classrooms nationwide, we have watched students' curiosity, confidence, and problem-solving skills grow as they tend plants in schools gardens, indoors and outside.

NGA's GrowLab™ program uses specially designed indoor classroom gardens as living laboratories to engage students in exploring science and a range of other subjects. The GrowLab Indoor Garden, Teachers Guide, and Curriculum help elementary and middle school teachers introduce garden-based, interdisciplinary learning activities that are both stimulating and fun.

Partnerships between schools and community organizations help youth gardening projects thrive. NGA works with an extensive network of educators, clubs, corporations, and resource people who provide assistance to school gardening programs. We are available to help you make these connections and find the best guidance and instructional materials available.

If you would like to receive information about membership, publications, and education programs of the National Gardening Association, please write to us at:

National Gardening Association
Youth Programs
180 Flynn Avenue
Burlington, Vermont 05401
(802) 863-1308

4388